SCOTT FORESMAN

SOCIAL STUDIES

MARYLAND

PEARSON

Scott
Foresman

Editorial Offices: Glenview, Illinois • Parsippany, New Jersey • New York, New York
Sales Offices: Boston, Massachusetts • Duluth, Georgia • Glenview, Illinois •
Coppell, Texas • Sacramento, California • Mesa, Arizona

www.sfsocialstudies.com

TEACHER REVIEWERS

Leslie Andrathy
Director Curriculum and Professional
  Development
Archdiocese of Baltimore
Baltimore, Maryland

Joshua L. Fradel
Coordinator of Instruction
Worcester County Public Schools
Newark, Maryland

Mary Ann Hewitt
Associate Executive Director
Maryland Council on Economic
  Education
Towson, Maryland

Susan Himmelheber
Elementary Teacher
St. John's School
Hollywood, Maryland

ISBN: 0-328-22269-0

Copyright © 2007, Pearson Education, Inc.

5 6 7 8 9 10 V052 14 13 12 11

Contents

Maryland

Maryland is "bathed in a singular and various beauty, from the stately estuaries of the Chesapeake to the peaks of the Blue Ridge."

—H.L. Mencken

Contents

Maryland

This engraving shows the State House in Annapolis, Maryland, in 1786. The State House was the location of the Annapolis Convention held in that year.

Maryland is "... bathed in a singular and various beauty, from the stately estuaries of the Chesapeake to the peaks of the Blue Ridge."

H.L. Mencken

Welcome to Maryland

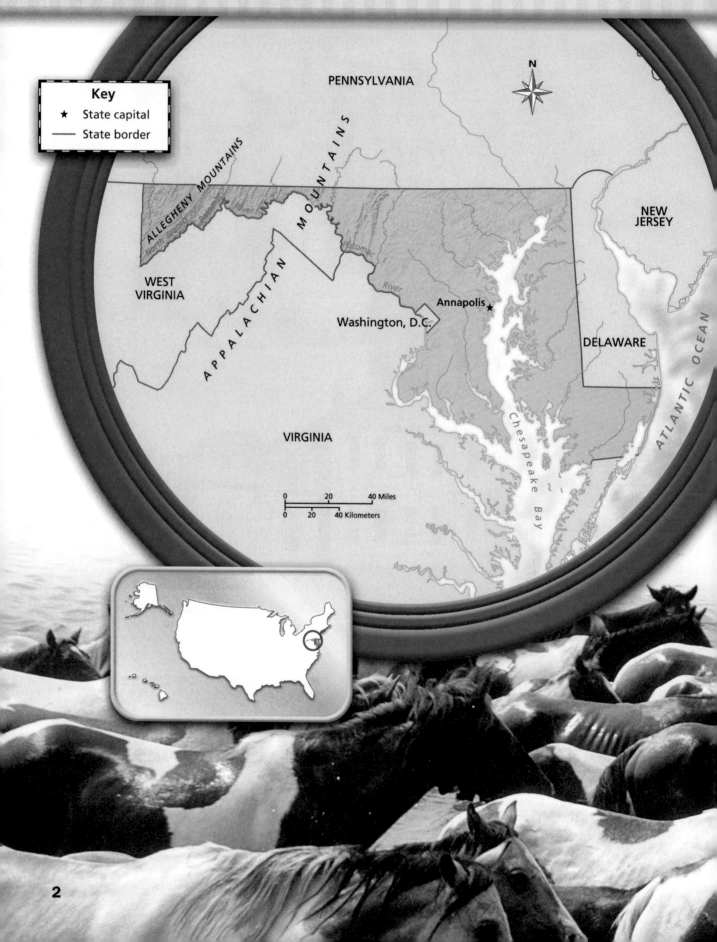

Key
★ State capital
— State border

PENNSYLVANIA

N

ALLEGHENY MOUNTAINS

North Branch

Potomac River

A P P A L A C H I A N   M O U N T A I N S

WEST VIRGINIA

Potomac

River

NEW JERSEY

Annapolis ★

Washington, D.C.

DELAWARE

VIRGINIA

Chesapeake Bay

ATLANTIC OCEAN

0   20   40 Miles
0   20   40 Kilometers

▶ Rolling hills and fertile valleys create rich farmland in the Piedmont Plateau.

▶ The blue crab is one of Maryland's state symbols.

▶ The historic city of Annapolis has been Maryland's state capital for more than 200 years.

▶ Places such as Black Rock in Maryland's Appalachian Mountain region offer recreation and beautiful views.

▶ The wild ponies of Assateague Island are a popular tourist attraction.

Reading Social Studies

Maryland
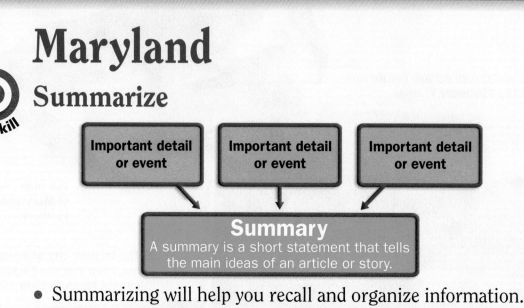

Summarize

| Important detail or event | Important detail or event | Important detail or event |

Summary
A summary is a short statement that tells the main ideas of an article or story.

- Summarizing will help you recall and organize information.
- Choose important details or events in an article or story.
- Leave out less important details or events.
- Use only a sentence or two in a summary.

A Fascinating and Diverse State

Maryland is a fascinating state. Its land is mountainous in the west, rolling to flat in the center, and low and wet in the east. Our state also has a long, rich history with a proud heritage and culture.

Maryland has many natural resources such as minerals, timber, marine life, and fertile soil. Its forests and waterways provide homes for plants and animals.

Maryland's role in history includes Native Americans, European settlers, and immigrants from around the world. These Marylanders have been involved in the struggles and successes of the entire nation.

Our state has a long tradition of music, art, literature, crafts, and sports. All of these enrich our state and our country.

Use the reading skill of summarizing to answer these questions.

1. What is the most important idea in paragraph two?
2. Which details in paragraph two would you leave out of a summary?
3. Write a brief summary of the passage.

The Geography of Maryland

CHAPTER 1

Lesson 1
Ocean City
Maryland has a variety of landforms and waterways.

Lesson 2
Appalachian Mountains
Maryland has three geographic regions.

Lesson 3
Salisbury
Maryland has many kinds of resources to help its economy.

Lesson 4
Rockville
Marylanders have many employment opportunities in areas such as science and government.

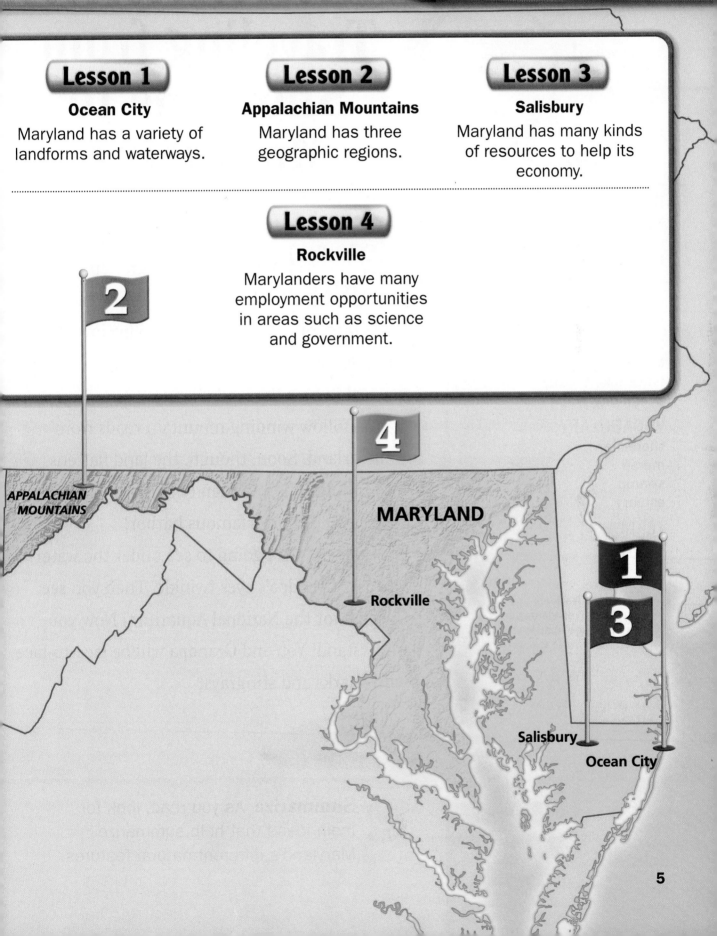

APPALACHIAN MOUNTAINS

MARYLAND

Rockville

Salisbury

Ocean City

MARYLAND

Marsh Mountain
Baltimore
Annapolis
Ocean City
Pocomoke Swamp

PREVIEW

Focus on the Main Idea
Maryland is a small state with many different kinds of landforms and waterways.

PLACES
Annapolis
Baltimore
Marsh Mountain
Pocomoke Swamp
Ocean City

VOCABULARY
shoreline
marsh
swamp
estuary

TERM
high-tech

▶ Baltimore's National Aquarium gives visitors a chance to see sharks and other underwater creatures.

Traveling from Shoreline to Mountains

You Are There

"Water is so important to life in Maryland," your grandpa says, "that I want you to see the life that's *under* the water, too." Grandpa loves surprises, and so do you! On your trip, you watch how the land changes.

You follow winding mountain roads from Cumberland. Soon, though, the land flattens into rolling hills and then to smooth, flat plains. You see Baltimore's famous harbor!

"But how am I going to see under the water?" you ask. Grandpa's eyes twinkle. Then you see the sign for the National Aquarium! Now you understand! You and Grandpa will be face-to-face with sharks and stingrays!

Summarize As you read, look for main ideas that help summarize Maryland's different natural features.

6

Borders and Capitals

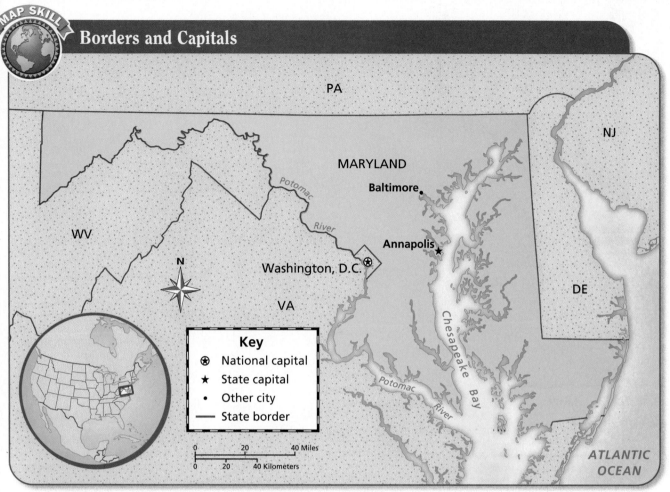

PA

MARYLAND

Baltimore.

Potomac

River

NJ

WV

N

Annapolis ★

Washington, D.C. ⊛

VA

DE

Chesapeake Bay

Key

⊛ National capital
★ State capital
• Other city
— State border

Potomac River

ATLANTIC
OCEAN

| 0 | | 20 | | 40 Miles |
| 0 | 20 | | 40 Kilometers | |

▶ **Maryland is located on important waterways.**

MAP SKILL Understand Borders *Which states border Maryland on the north?*

Maryland's Location and Features

Maryland's location is special—it is in the middle of the Atlantic coastline halfway between Florida and Maine.

Maryland borders Pennsylvania, Virginia, Delaware, West Virginia, Washington, D.C., and the Atlantic Ocean.

You can see by looking at the map that the Chesapeake Bay divides Maryland into eastern and western areas, each with a **shoreline,** or the line where land and water meet. Most of Maryland's rivers empty into the bay.

Many of our state's largest cities are located on the bay's western shore.

Being near the water gives people job opportunities, beautiful views, and many kinds of water activities.

Annapolis, Maryland's capital, is historic. Once known as Anne Arundel Town, it became Maryland's capital in 1695.

Baltimore, one of the nation's busiest seaports, has the largest population of any city in the state. A Baltimore mayor once called Baltimore "Charm City" because of its many different neighborhoods, people, and cultures. Visitors from around the world visit Baltimore's National Aquarium.

REVIEW Summarize the features that make Maryland's location special.
↻ **Summarize**

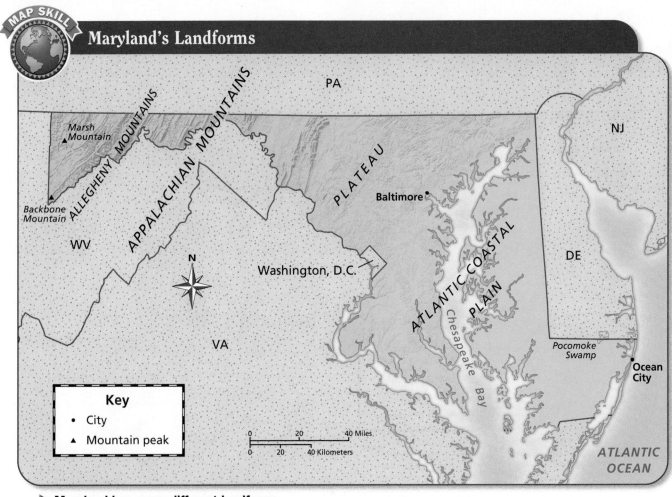

PA

Marsh
Mountain ▲

ALLEGHENY MOUNTAINS

APPALACHIAN MOUNTAINS

Backbone
Mountain ▲

WV

NJ

PLATEAU

Baltimore •

N

Washington, D.C.

DE

VA

ATLANTIC COASTAL PLAIN

Chesapeake Bay

Pocomoke
Swamp

Ocean
City

Key
- • City
- ▲ Mountain peak

0   20   40 Miles
0   20   40 Kilometers

ATLANTIC
OCEAN

▶ **Maryland has many different landforms.**

MAP SKILL Understand Landforms *Name three landforms found in Maryland.*

A Small but Varied Land

Your trip from Maryland's mountains to the National Aquarium in Baltimore might not have taken as long as you thought it would. Maryland is a small state. In fact, only eight states are smaller. A point near Hancock, Maryland, is less than two miles wide. You can walk across the state there in about thirty minutes!

Few states, though, have so many different kinds of land. Marylanders can hike in mountain forests, visit a thoroughbred horse farm on the plateau, and end their day with a tasty crab dinner at the shore.

Maryland's land rises from sea level on the Atlantic Coast to 3,360 feet at Backbone Mountain in the Allegheny Mountains. In the winter people ski and snowboard on **Marsh Mountain.** Throughout the year, they can explore national forests and parks. Maryland's many lakes and rivers are perfect for boating and swimming on hot summer days.

Just east of the mountains, the land is a narrow plateau region. There, Maryland's farmers have rich soil and plenty of water to grow many different kinds of crops. Growing crops is an important part of Maryland's economy.

Closer to the bay, the land becomes a coastal plain—flat, low land that is also good for farming. In some places, **marshes,** watery areas covered in miles of grass, are ideal homes for wildlife. Marshes are great places for bird watching!

Exploring the **Pocomoke Swamp** is also a wonderful adventure. A **swamp** is like a marsh, but instead of grasses, tall trees like the bald cypress grow in the shallow water. Maryland also has many other kinds of trees because of its varied land and climate.

Maryland's Chesapeake Bay is one of the state's most valuable treasures. People fish and harvest crabs, clams, and oysters in its waters. Tourists come to many bay towns as well as **Ocean City** on the Atlantic coast. They enjoy the beaches, water sports, and delicious seafood.

Like everything else about Maryland, the state's climate has something for everyone. In the eastern part of the state, the winters are often mild, with rain and only a few inches of snow. But in the Appalachian Mountains, winter may bring nearly seven feet of snow and freezing temperatures each year. In the hot, humid summers, Marylanders often cool off in mountain lakes and campgrounds.

REVIEW Write a brief summary of Maryland's landforms. ↻ Summarize

FACT FILE

Maryland's Climate

Maryland's climate changes by season and location. The lowland areas have much warmer weather than the higher mountain areas. Look at the map and graph to learn more about Maryland's climate.

Average Monthly Precipitation

3.35 inches per month

3.54 inches per month

MARYLAND

Key
- Western Mountains
- Central
- Southern
- Eastern Shore

3.3 inches per month

3.48 inches per month

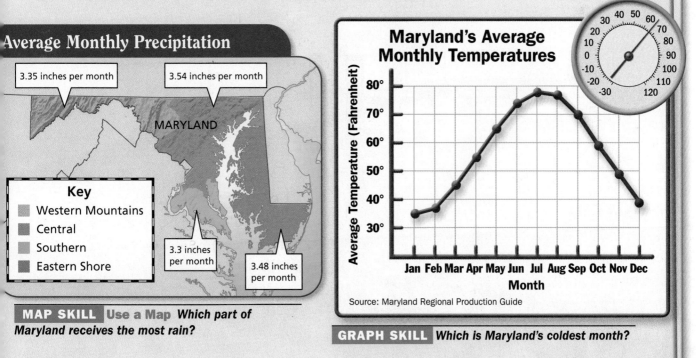

Maryland's Average Monthly Temperatures

Average Temperature (Fahrenheit)

Jan Feb Mar Apr May Jun Jul Aug Sep Oct Nov Dec

Month

Source: Maryland Regional Production Guide

MAP SKILL Use a Map *Which part of Maryland receives the most rain?*

GRAPH SKILL *Which is Maryland's coldest month?*

9

Waterways, Railroads, and Highways

You have read about Maryland's different landforms. Each of them has shaped the ways Marylanders travel and communicate with others.

Maryland's rivers flow through the state and connect with larger waterways such as Chesapeake Bay. This bay is an **estuary** (ES choo air ee), a coastal waterway in which fresh river water and seawater mix. It is open to the Atlantic Ocean, but many rivers supply it with freshwater.

The bay, the largest estuary in the United States, is a gateway for trade. At Baltimore's port, ships load and unload cargo from around the world, and smaller boats use the bay's waters for work and play.

When the Chesapeake Bay Bridge opened in 1952, people could drive across

▶ **Ships from around the world are loaded and unloaded in Baltimore's harbor.**

the bay from Maryland's eastern shore to its western shore for the first time. Now, more than 20 million cars cross the bridge every year. Each year, thousands of people gather to participate in the annual "Bridge Walk" across the bay.

▶ **The Chesapeake Bay Bridge is one of the world's longest bridges.**

Hundreds of years ago, people in Maryland traveled mostly by water. Transportation was slow and difficult. About 200 years ago, Marylanders started building roads to make travel easier. They also built canals for travel and transporting goods. The Chesapeake and Delaware Canal was built in soggy marshland all the way between Delaware River and Chesapeake Bay!

Maryland also had the first American railroad. The B&O Railroad carried goods to and from Baltimore's harbor. Today the CSX Transportation system carries products in the state.

Today almost 30,000 miles of highway connect Maryland's cities and towns with one another and with other states. The Fort McHenry Tunnel even takes cars under the water of Baltimore Harbor! Air

▶ After several railroads joined together in 1986, the CSX transportation system provided freight service in Maryland.

travel and **high-tech,** or advanced, communication networks link Maryland to the rest of the world.

REVIEW Summarize some ways Marylanders travel and transport goods.
🔁 Summarize

Summarize the Lesson

- **Maryland's location is in the middle of the Atlantic coastline, halfway between Maine and Florida.**

- **Maryland has a variety of landforms and waterways that make it an ideal place to work and live.**

- **Maryland's transportation and communication network includes waterways, railroads, and highways.**

LESSON 1 REVIEW

Check Facts and Main Ideas

1. 🔁 Summarize On a sheet of paper, fill in the diagram to show how Maryland has a variety of natural features.

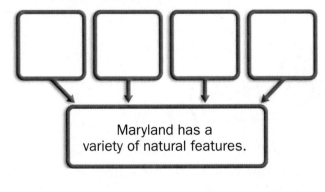

Maryland has a variety of natural features.

2. Describe Maryland's location in the United States.

3. How does Maryland's variety of landforms and waterways create jobs?

4. What forms of transportation move goods and people in Maryland?

5. **Critical Thinking:** *Draw Conclusions* Why do you think Maryland's major cities developed near water?

Link to ○○ Writing

Write a Report Use the library or the Internet to research a report about an important landform in your area. How was it formed? Why is it important to the people in your community?

MARYLAND

APPALACHIAN MTS.
PIEDMONT PLATEAU
DELMARVA PLAIN
ATLANTIC COASTAL
PENINSULA

PREVIEW

Focus on the Main Idea
Maryland has three very
different geographic regions.

PLACES
Atlantic Coastal Plain
Piedmont Plateau
Appalachian Mountains
Delmarva Peninsula

VOCABULARY
piedmont

TERMS
fall line
mountain system

▶ Grab your snowboard and
head for Maryland's Marsh
Mountain.

Maryland's Regions

> **You Are There**

Your parents really surprised you
this year! Your new snowboard is
your favorite birthday gift.

As your family packs, you hear on the radio
that almost a foot of new snow has fallen in
the mountains. That's just the kind of snow a
beginning snowboarder needs—deep and soft.
Your parents are going cross-country skiing,
and your sister is going to downhill ski with
her friend. But you are having your first
snowboarding lesson with an expert instructor!

Just think. You could have gone ice fishing
on Deep Creek Lake with your friend and his
parents. Brrrrr!

Summarize As you read, look for
details that will help you summarize
the differences among Maryland's
three geographic regions.

Target Skill

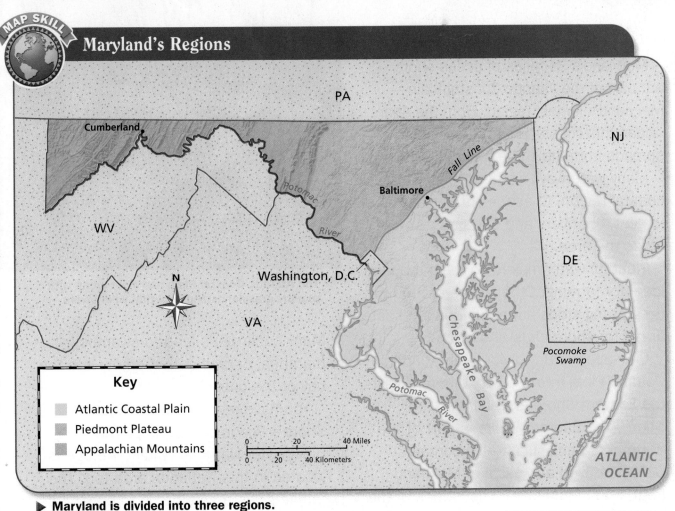

Key

- Atlantic Coastal Plain
- Piedmont Plateau
- Appalachian Mountains

0   20   40 Miles

0   20   40 Kilometers

► **Maryland is divided into three regions.**

MAP SKILL Use a Map *Which region borders the ocean?*

Maryland's Regions

Geographers divide Maryland into three regions. Each region has unique physical features. Because Maryland is a small state, many Marylanders live in one region and work in another.

Maryland's **Atlantic Coastal Plain** region covers more than half the state. This low, flat land near the ocean is split by Chesapeake Bay. Some of the land is close to sea level and spongy with water. Birds make their homes there. Yet in this same region, large cities, such as Baltimore, are home to most Marylanders.

The **Piedmont Plateau** region in the center of the state is higher than the land near the shore but lower than the western mountains. When rivers reach the edge of the plateau, they drop down in rushing waterfalls. The area where rivers form waterfalls or rapids because of a drop in the land's elevation is the **fall line.** Baltimore became a great port city because the fall line kept ships from going farther up the rivers.

The **Appalachian Mountain** region is the highest part of the state. In this region black bears still live in the mountain forests, and people grow delicious fruits in its valleys. It is a great region to try out your new snowboard or skis!

REVIEW Summarize Maryland's geographic regions. ↻ **Summarize**

Atlantic Coastal Plain

Maryland's 31 miles of ocean shore are part of the Atlantic Coastal Plain— Maryland's largest region. From the Atlantic Ocean this coastal plain, or low land, spreads from the shore to the fall line.

Many waterways weave through this coastal region. Chesapeake Bay is the largest, but rivers and streams also cross the area.

Plentiful water makes some of the land ideal for farming. Other areas are too wet for growing crops but make beautiful safe areas for shore birds and animals.

Chesapeake Bay divides the Atlantic Coastal Plain into two very different parts, the Eastern Shore and the Western Shore. The Eastern Shore is part of the Delmarva Peninsula which contains Delaware (Del) and parts of Maryland (mar) and Virginia (va). The names of the states make up the name *Delmarva.* Much of the peninsula is wet and marshy.

▶ **The Atlantic Coastal Plain has open areas with marshy grasslands and beautiful wildflowers.**

Many back roads lead to swamps, marshes, or creeks that empty into the bay or the ocean.

You have read about the Eastern Shore's Pocomoke Swamp. The Blackwater National Wildlife Refuge is located in this wetlands area too. The refuge gives a safe home to endangered birds such as the bald eagle and peregrine falcon.

▶ **Baltimore is located where the Atlantic Coastal Plain meets the fall line. Its harbor has become one of America's most important ports.**

Many people who live on the Eastern Shore make their living by fishing, harvesting shellfish, or building ships. After the Chesapeake Bay Bridge opened, tourists came in greater numbers to enjoy the beaches and beautiful natural areas. Boats shove off from the Eastern Shore to catch some of the bay's 200 varieties of fish.

The Western Shore of the Atlantic Coastal Plain is slightly higher than the Eastern Shore. The Western Shore has fewer wetlands than the Eastern Shore, and more farms are located in the upper Eastern Shore area.

The first European settlement in Maryland began on the Western Shore at

▶ Chesapeake Bay is home to the diamondback terrapin, a sea turtle. It used to be hunted for its meat but is now protected. Today, wild terps leave their little tracks on the beaches of the Eastern Shore.

Changes Through Time *Many scientists believe that millions of years ago, a warm shallow sea covered all of southern Maryland. Today, at Calvert Cliffs State Park, people can find fossils including ancient shark teeth.*

St. Mary's City. When the first colonists arrived, they saw a flat land covered with forests of huge oak and pine trees. Today the Western Shore still has more trees than the Eastern Shore.

People on the Western Shore, like most Marylanders, depend on waterways. The Potomac River, one of the region's famous rivers, provides Marylanders with seafood, recreation, education, and a water route to larger bodies of water. The region's charter fishing fleet takes sport fishers all the way out to the Atlantic Ocean!

REVIEW In what ways is the Eastern Shore different from the Western Shore of the Atlantic Coastal Plain?
Compare and Contrast

▶ **Farms on the Piedmont Plateau enjoy four seasons of mostly moderate weather.**

Piedmont Plateau

The Piedmont Plateau is Maryland's middle region. The word **piedmont** means "at the foot of a mountain," which is exactly where this region is located. To the west, the Appalachian Mountain region borders the plateau.

At the fall line, the lands of the plateau fall off to the plain below, turning rivers and streams into cascades of white water. Between the lands at the foot of the mountains and the fall line, the Piedmont Plateau has low rolling hills and fertile river valleys. You can see old-fashioned covered bridges at several streams or river crossings.

The Potomac, which forms Maryland's southern border, flows through this region. When it reaches the fall line, the Great Falls drop roaring white water into the coastal plain below. Some brave kayakers test their skill by riding over the falls!

The region's Bush River Basin is another good example of how rivers flow through the Piedmont Plateau. Many smaller streams and creeks feed into the Bush River as it brings water to the region's forests and farmland. Trout and other fish live in its waters, and people enjoy boating and fishing there.

▶ **The Great Falls on the Potomac River mark the fall line between the Piedmont Plateau region and the Atlantic Coastal Plain region.**

Below the fall line, the Bush River adds its freshwater to the Chesapeake Bay estuary.

Fertile land and plenty of water make the Piedmont Plateau region ideal for growing crops. Here, some farmers grow food crops, such as soybeans, oats, and corn. Others grow plants and flowers that people buy for their homes and gardens.

Still others grow food for animals, such as dairy and beef cattle. Dairy farms dot the countryside. Delicious milk, other dairy products, and beef come from cattle raised on Piedmont Plateau grasses.

Changes Through Time *The Piedmont Plateau region was the setting for several Civil War events. Today tourists come to the area to visit these historical sites.*

▶ **According to legend Barbara Fritchie bravely waved the Union flag in front of Stonewall Jackson and his Confederate army during the Civil War.**

▶ **The Baltimore Oriole, Maryland's state bird, often lives in forests and thickets.**

People outside of Maryland are often surprised to learn how many horse farms there are in the Piedmont Plateau region. Raising and racing horses has been an important part of Maryland's history. This fertile region with its rolling hills and rich grasslands is a great place for a thoroughbred to grow and train for the next big race.

REVIEW What do the Piedmont Plateau and the Atlantic Coastal Plain have in common? **Compare and Contrast**

17

Map Adventure

Maryland's Mountain Activities

Map labels: Frostburg · Cumberland · Hagerstown · MARYLAND · McHenry · Deep Creek Lake · Western Mountain Scenic Railroad · Backbone Mountain · Chesapeake and Ohio National Park · Potomac River

Legend:
- Cities
- Railroads
- Canals
- Highways

0   10   20 miles

N W E S

Use the map to help plan a family trip.

1. Where is the Chesapeake and Ohio Canal Festival located?

2. What direction is the Western Maryland Blues Festival from the Canal Festival?

3. Where might you stop to take a boat ride if you were traveling from the Backbone Mountain to the arts festival?

Some May Festivals	
Festivals	**Place**
Chesapeake & Ohio Canal Festival	Cumberland
Garret Lakes Arts Festival	McHenry
Western Maryland Blues Festival	Hagerstown

Appalachian Mountains

The Appalachian Mountain region has three different mountain groups. The region gets its name from the larger Appalachian Mountain range, which runs along the eastern coast of the United States. In the western region of Maryland, the Allegheny Mountains and the Blue Ridge Mountains join the Appalachians to form a mountain system of beautiful mountain ridges, meadows, and valleys.

The Allegheny Mountains rise in the far western area of Maryland. The Blue Ridge Mountains are located closer to the Piedmont Plateau. They get their name from the blue haze that hangs above their thick forests. The Appalachian system spreads across Maryland's western corner.

The Appalachian Mountain region has little flat land for farming in the far western section. Between the Blue Ridge and Allegheny Mountains, though, mountain rains provide water for fruit orchards in the valley.

Changes Through Time *In the 1800s Cumberland was the last stop for travelers riding a boat on the Chesapeake and Ohio Canal from Washington, D.C. Today the canal runs through the Chesapeake and Ohio National Historic Park.*

Waterways in the Appalachian Mountain region are fast-moving mountain streams and rivers. One part of the Youghiogheny (yah kuh GAY nee) River, nicknamed the Yough (yahk) River, became Maryland's first "wild" river. To protect the environment, logging and development are not allowed on parts of the riverbanks. Outdoor adventurers ride the wild river in kayaks and rafts.

This region also has many lakes. You read that people go ice fishing in Deep Creek Lake. Some people also scuba dive there, looking for treasures in sunken farmhouses. The homes were covered with water in the 1920s when the lake formed behind a dam on the Yough River.

In this rugged region, you are always near a state park or forest. The cool, deep forests bring welcome relief from summer heat. The town of Cumberland, located east of Deep Creek Lake, has year-round outdoor activities.

▶ This Cumberland steam engine takes visitors along on an 11-mile scenic route through modern Maryland.

REVIEW What makes the Appalachian Mountain region different from any other region in Maryland? Compare and Contrast

Summarize the Lesson

- **Maryland has three geographic regions.**
- **The Atlantic Coastal Plain region is in the southeastern part of Maryland.**
- **The Piedmont Plateau region is in the central part of Maryland.**
- **The Appalachian Mountain region is in the western part of Maryland.**

LESSON 2 REVIEW

Check Facts and Main Ideas

1. ⟳ Summarize On a separate sheet of paper, fill in the diagram with the name and description of each region.

Maryland's regions have a variety of activities and occupations.

2. Where is each of Maryland's three regions located?

3. In what ways is water important to each region?

4. Describe one way that each region has changed over time.

5. **Critical Thinking: *Cause and Effect*** Identify each region's natural resources and explain how they help Marylanders earn a living.

Link to ➙∞⟵ Science

Research at the library and on the Internet to find out why it is important to take good care of wetland environments. Make a list of three things people can do to keep wetlands healthy.

MARYLAND

Wye Mills•
Salisbury•
Crisfield•

PREVIEW

Focus on the Main Idea
Maryland has many kinds of economic activities because of its varied resources.

PLACES
Crisfield
Salisbury
Wye Mills

VOCABULARY
watershed
habitat
deforestation

TERM
tree community

▶ A day on a skipjack can be an exciting adventure.

Maryland's Resources

You Are There
Your cousin, Alex, is visiting from Utah! Today you and he are going out on a skipjack boat in Chesapeake Bay. As you set sail, the captain tells you why he likes to take people out on the bay. "Commercial watermen work hard," he says. "I want people to see where their seafood dinners come from!"

Out on the bay, you and Alex see different kinds of boats. Some watermen use nets to bring in fish. On one boat the crew lowers pots to catch crabs and eels. Boats with dredges scoop up clams. Sailing on a skipjack is great fun, but now you know what hard work fishing for a living is.

"See those people with a line and a pole," you say. "They must be vacation-fishing!"

Summarize As you read, think of ways to summarize how Maryland's resources make its economy strong.

▶ Baltimore's port is one of the busiest in America. Goods are unloaded and loaded for a world market.

▶ Oysters are an important harvest from Maryland's waters.

Water Resources

Suppose that it is Labor Day weekend. You dock your boat in the small Eastern Shore town of **Crisfield.** It is time for the National Hard Crab Derby and Fair. Music is playing. Crabs are cooking. Soon you will watch a crab race. Marylanders call Crisfield the "Seafood Capital of the World."

The rich fishing resources of Chesapeake Bay have always brought work and food to Marylanders. The bay area has thousands of kinds of oysters, crabs, fish, and other animals and plants.

The bay also helps transport resources to buyers. In 2000 the port of Baltimore loaded and unloaded more than 40 million tons of goods from all around the world.

Maryland's rivers are also an important water resource. You learned that rivers create many waterfalls at the fall line where the plateau falls off to the coastal plain. Generators turn the power of the falling water into electricity. The Conowingo (kah nuh WIN goh) Dam on Maryland's Susquehanna (suhs kwuh HAN nuh) River is one of the biggest hydroelectric power producers in America. Hydroelectric power is water-generated electricity.

Water also brings tourists to Maryland. They boat, fish, swim, and raft on Maryland's white water rivers and enjoy the state's beaches.

REVIEW Summarize the benefits Maryland receives from its water resources. ↻ Summarize

Maryland's Products

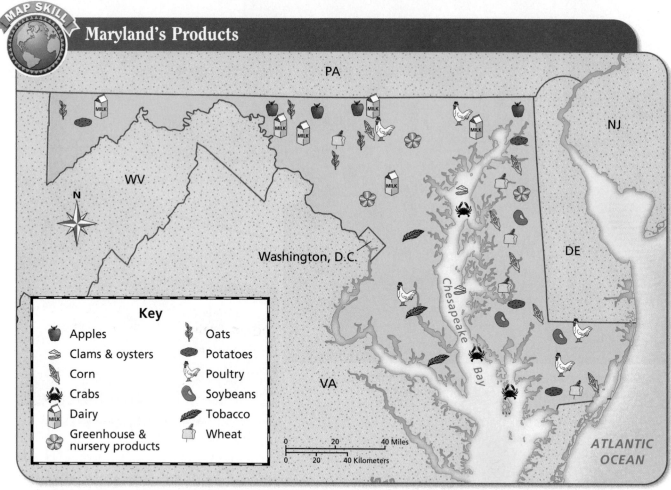

Key

- 🍎 Apples
- 🦪 Clams & oysters
- 🌿 Corn
- 🦀 Crabs
- 🥛 Dairy
- 🌸 Greenhouse & nursery products
- 🌾 Oats
- 🥔 Potatoes
- 🐔 Poultry
- 🫘 Soybeans
- 🌿 Tobacco
- 🌾 Wheat

0   20   40 Miles

0   20   40 Kilometers

▶ **Marylanders earn income from different products in different parts of the state.**

MAP SKILL Use a Product Map *What product is found mainly in south central Maryland?*

Fertile Land

You have learned that Maryland is a small state with many waterways and mountains. However, there is still plenty of land for producing farm products.

More than two million acres of Maryland is farmland. Greenhouse and nursery crops, such as flowers, shrubs, and young fruit trees, earn the most money for Maryland growers.

Other farms grow food. If you go to a local farmers' market in central Maryland during the early summer, you can buy strawberries. Later in the season you will find sweet corn, Maryland's most important vegetable crop.

You have read about mountain valleys filled with the scent of blossoming fruit trees in the spring. Later, Marylanders harvest their most important fruit crop from these orchards—apples! Think about how good fresh apple pies smell in the fall!

Maryland fruit growers are also proud of their other crops. Along with the many kinds of apples, fruit growers harvest peaches, pears, cherries, and berries.

Farm animals and animal products are the largest source of Maryland's farm income, however. Broilers, or chickens used for food, contribute the largest share.

Chickens are big business in the area around **Salisbury,** Maryland. Inland from the bay, Salisbury has become the largest city on the Eastern Shore because of nearby poultry farms. Some chickens provide eggs, but most are raised for their meat.

Maryland's farmers also raise cattle. After chickens, milk from dairy cows is the second-largest source of farm income in Maryland. Your last ice cream cone may have started out on one of Maryland's dairy farms! Other farm animals raised in Maryland are beef cattle, hogs, sheep, and horses.

Whether it is peaches or corn or soybeans, Maryland's fertile soil, climate, and water resources make it ideal for farming. Thousands of Marylanders make their living by farming and preparing farm products for shipping around the world.

The Maryland Department of Agriculture reports that for every Maryland farmer who produces farm products, there are about 10 other people who have jobs related to agriculture. Maryland's fertile land is important to everyone.

REVIEW What are some of the different farm products raised in Maryland?
Main Idea and Details

FACT FILE

Maryland Agriculture

Maryland's farmers try to find ways to grow better crops and take good care of the environment. Organizations such as the Beltsville Agricultural Research Center (BARC) use science to fight plant diseases and make fruits and vegetables even more delicious.

▶ Beltsville Agricultural Research Center (BARC) provides farmers with up-to-date research information.

▶ Maryland dairy farms raise healthy cows for delicious milk.

▶ Tomatoes are an important farm crop in Maryland.

▶ Corn crops produce a large share of Maryland's farm income.

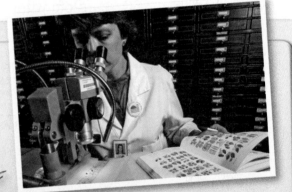

Forests

Most people in Maryland live less than an hour away from some of the state's forests. Almost half of Maryland is covered with trees. The mountains of western Maryland have more forests than any other Maryland region, but each region has its own kinds of trees. In the Atlantic Coastal Plain, the mild climate is just right for cypress trees. The higher mountains have oak and hardwood forests.

More than 150 kinds of trees are native to Maryland. Maryland's white oaks can grow up to 150 feet high. The famous Wye Oak in the town of **Wye Mills** was named the Maryland state tree in 1941. It was more than 460 years old when a thunderstorm destroyed it in 2002. That means it was growing in Maryland long before Maryland was even a state!

Forests are an important resource. They clean the air and keep fertile soil from washing away. They provide cool shade and homes for many animals and plants. They also provide lumber to build furniture and make paper. People in Maryland need to take good care of their forest resources.

Like people, trees live in communities. A **tree community** includes all of the different trees that live in an area because of their need for certain types of weather and soil. Maryland's forest managers watch for changes in water, soil, climate, animal life, or insects that might harm the tree community.

▶ **Many people in Maryland enjoy the state's parks and forests. Here the path takes hikers near a lock on the Chesapeake and Ohio canal.**

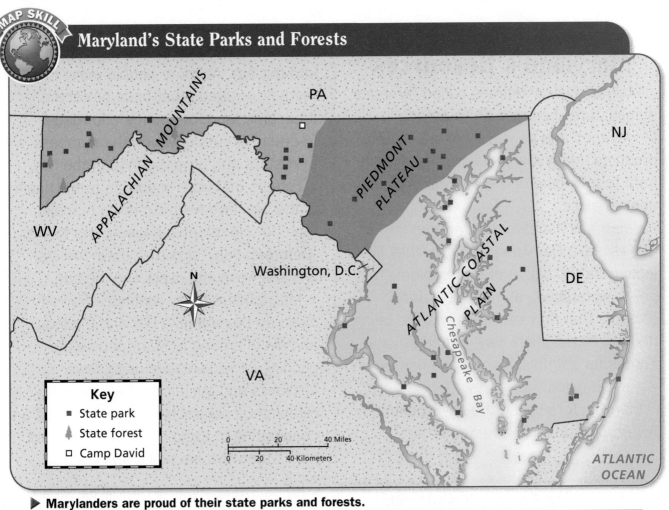

▶ Marylanders are proud of their state parks and forests.

MAP SKILL Use a Map *How many state parks are located in the Appalachian Mountain region?*

At one time, Maryland had about twice as much forestland as it does today. As European settlers came to Maryland, they cleared land for farming and for lumber to build houses.

Today logging, or cutting trees, is still important in Maryland's economy. Lumber and other forest products, such as maple syrup, Christmas trees, and paper, add more than one billion dollars each year to Maryland's economy. Thousands of Marylanders have jobs in forest industries.

REVIEW Summarize the ways in which forests are important to Maryland.
🔄 Summarize

▶ Camp David in Maryland's wooded Catoctin Mountain Park is a presidential vacation site. Here President George W. Bush walks with British Prime Minister Tony Blair.

Taking Care of Maryland's Resources

Maryland is sometimes called "America in miniature" because of its different landscapes and its variety of agricultural products. Many Marylanders are working hard to take care of the resources of this special place.

When Marylanders realized that Chesapeake Bay was in trouble, they first looked for the cause of the problem. The bay's **watershed,** all the rivers and streams that flow into the bay, were being harmed by pollution. Bay **habitats,** or homes for animals, plants, and fish, were in danger.

Many factors cause the bay's pollution. Rivers pick up fertilizers and other chemicals as they pass farms and factories. Then they empty their waters into the bay. As more people move near the bay, wetlands that once protected it become land for houses and roads. Overfishing cuts down on the numbers of oysters and other sea life in the bay.

Forests that were important to the health of the bay have been cut down to make room for more farms, houses, and towns. **Deforestation,** or cutting down forests, lets soil wash into rivers and the bay.

Marylanders today continue efforts to clean up Chesapeake Bay and the land and rivers around it. Many people are pitching in! Farmers are using fewer fertilizers and chemicals. People are cleaning up natural habitats and states are cooperating to avoid overfishing. Forests near waterways are being replanted.

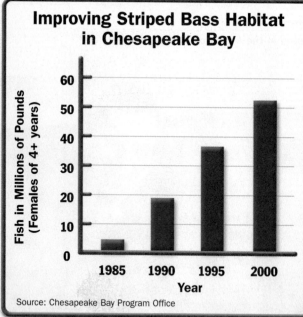

Improving Striped Bass Habitat in Chesapeake Bay

Fish in Millions of Pounds (Females of 4+ years)

0 — 10 — 20 — 30 — 40 — 50 — 60

1985 1990 1995 2000

Year

Source: Chesapeake Bay Program Office

▶ One way to judge how clean the water in Chesapeake Bay has become is to count the fish living there.

GRAPH SKILL *About how much did the striped bass population increase between 1985 and 2000?*

▶ People of all ages work to clean up the bay, but it will take much more work to make it clean and safe for wildlife.

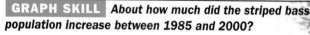

Marylanders are working together to care for their resources, and now parts of Chesapeake Bay are safe for fishing and swimming.

REVIEW How have Marylanders cooperated to care for the state's natural resources. ↻ Summarize

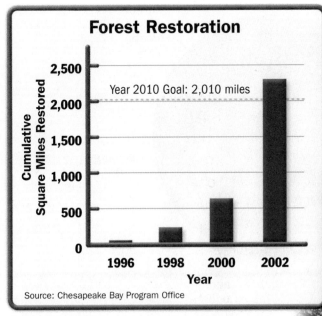

Forest Restoration

Year 2010 Goal: 2,010 miles

Source: Chesapeake Bay Program Office

▶ **Marylanders passed their goal for the year 2010 in 2002.**

GRAPH SKILL *What year on the graph is the lowest point for forest restoration?*

Summarize the Lesson

- **Maryland's water resources are important to its economy.**

- **Fertile land makes farming possible in many parts of the state.**

- **Maryland's forests create jobs and recreation for Marylanders.**

- **People in Maryland are working together to preserve their state resources.**

▶ **Forest resources need to be protected to provide habitats for plants and animals.**

LESSON 3   REVIEW

Check Facts and Main Ideas

1. ↻ Summarize On a separate sheet of paper, fill in the diagram to summarize how each listed resource is used in an economic activity.

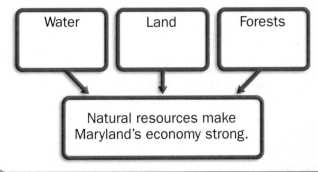

| Water | Land | Forests |

Natural resources make Maryland's economy strong.

2. What are some important economic activities on Chesapeake Bay?

3. What plants produce the largest share of Maryland's income from crops?

4. How has cooperation among Maryland's people improved Chesapeake Bay?

5. **Critical Thinking:** *Cause and Effect* What causes pollution in Chesapeake Bay?

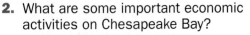

Link to ⫯⫯ **Writing**

Write a Letter Write a letter to a friend about the ways people are trying to clean up Chesapeake Bay.

Read a Circle Graph

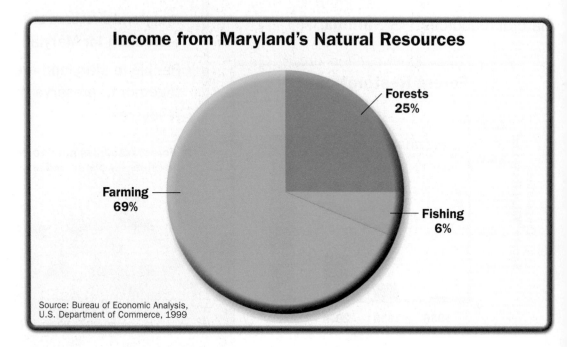

Income from Maryland's Natural Resources

- Forests 25%
- Fishing 6%
- Farming 69%

Source: Bureau of Economic Analysis,
U.S. Department of Commerce, 1999

What? Graphs are useful tools because they show information at a glance. Suppose that you want to know which of Maryland's natural resources creates the largest percentage of income for Marylanders. You could read reports about the resources to find information. Then you could figure out which resource had the highest dollar value and work out percentages.

If you use a circle graph, though, you can see the information all at once. The whole circle shows natural resources, and each "slice" of the circle shows a specific kind of resource. The circle graph here shows the percentage of total income from natural resources earned from each resource.

▶ **Logging is an important part of Maryland's forestry economy.**

Why? Knowing how to read graphs can help you understand information and see the relationships among facts quickly. Creating graphs about information you are reading is another way for you to understand it. Using the graph on page 28 will help you summarize the importance of our state's natural resources and understand why caring for them is important to Maryland.

How? To use a circle graph, first look at the title. Then read the words in the graph to learn what each section represents. In this circle graph, each section represents one of Maryland's resources, and the percentages represent the part of the total income that the different resources produce in 1999.

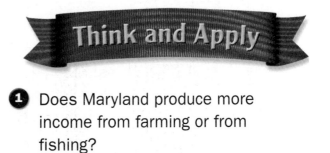

Think and Apply

1 Does Maryland produce more income from farming or from fishing?

2 What percentage of income does Maryland make from forest products?

3 Which resource produces the most income for Maryland?

▶ **Farming income is important to Maryland's economy.**

Improving Maryland's Water

What do you care about? Bernie Fowler cares deeply about Maryland's waterways. He wants Maryland's rivers to become as clean as they were before pollution started clouding their clear water and harming wildlife.

People in Maryland also want to know whether the waters of Chesapeake Bay are getting cleaner. Former Senator Bernie Fowler has found a way to do just that with something called a "wade-in."

More than 50 years ago, Bernie Fowler used to go crabbing in the Patuxent River. The Patuxent is the longest river that is located completely within Maryland. It flows between Washington, D.C., and Baltimore and then into Chesapeake Bay. When Bernie Fowler waded into the river, the water was so clean that he could see not only crabs and fish but his toes too! In the years that followed, though, pollution made the water cloudy and dark. So he decided to run an experiment.

▶ People of all ages join Bernie Fowler at the wade-in.

BUILDING
CITIZENSHIP
★ Caring
Respect
Responsibility
Fairness
Honesty
Courage

In 1986 Bernie Fowler put on his white sneakers, overalls, and a farm hat. Then he waded chest-deep into the river to see whether he could see his white tennis shoes. Each year after that, more people joined him. Now the wade-in is also happening in many other Maryland waterways. People are checking for themselves to see that their waterways are getting cleaner.

Bernie Fowler has seen improvement over the years. Here's how he keeps track of changes in how clear the water is. He wades out as far as he can and stops when he can no longer see his white sneakers through the murky water. He measures the watermark on his overalls. The higher the mark, the clearer the water is that year.

Caring in Action

Link to Current Events Marylanders care about their state and want to keep it beautiful. Make a list of the things you could do in your community to show that you care about Maryland. Compare your list with those of your classmates. Which suggestions would make a good class project?

LESSON 4

MARYLAND

Rockville • • Greenbelt
Washington,
D.C.

Chesapeake
Bay

PREVIEW

Focus on the Main Idea
Because of Maryland's economic diversity, people have opportunities in many different kinds of jobs.

PLACES
Washington, D.C.
Greenbelt
Rockville
Chesapeake Bay

VOCABULARY
longshoreman

TERM
service industry

▶ Many Marylanders work at the Baltimore Zoo taking care of animals, teaching people about conservation, and serving the public.

Working in Maryland

You Are There "You're back!" says Jamie, your favorite instructor at Zoo Summer Camp at the Baltimore Zoo. Jamie remembers you from last year, but this year is different. You're going behind the scenes with the animals! Campers must be at least fourth graders for this special treat.

You follow Jamie to a place meant only for people who work at the zoo. Back here, animal keepers clean the cages and prepare food for the animals.

"Jamie, I want to work at the zoo when I grow up," you say. Jamie explains that you can apply for a job as a camp instructor when you're 18. But if you want to be a zoo veterinarian, you will need much more education. You know you can do it!

Summarize As you read, look for main ideas that will help you summarize the ways people in Maryland earn a living.

Maryland's Economy

You have read about Maryland's many resources—its fertile land, waterways, transportation links, and its nearly perfect location near **Washington, D.C.** These resources helped Maryland's economy become one of the country's strongest.

In this chapter you will read about another important part of Maryland's economy—its people. Marylanders hold a wide variety of jobs. They buy and sell products and move them around the country and the world. They develop new technologies. Most important, they provide services to other Marylanders and to the rest of the United States.

If your class of about 25 students represented all of Maryland, 17 of your classmates would work in the **service industry,** or jobs that provide services to others. Many of the service jobs would be in either education or medicine. About 3 of the 17 jobs would provide services in retail business. Your 17 classmates could be doctors, lawyers, sales clerks, teachers, researchers, bus drivers, or business people.

Because they have important jobs, Marylanders must be well trained—and they are! Maryland has some of the best-educated workers in the United States. It also ranks first in the percentage of professional and technical workers in a single state.

REVIEW Describe some of the ways that people in Maryland earn a living.
↺ **Summarize**

Making a Living in Maryland

Other
0.3%

Jobs in
Government
18.3%

Jobs Providing Services
67.4%

Jobs Producing
Goods
14%

GRAPH SKILL *What kinds of jobs might be included in the 14% segment in the circle graph?*

▶ People in Maryland work in many different kinds of jobs, including research, nursing, and food preparation.

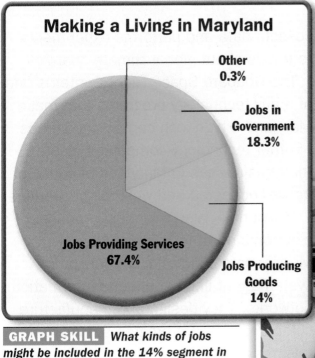

33

▶ **The in-flight data sent back from Goddard's unmanned spacecraft help technicians monitor global climate changes.**

Working in Technology

Maryland's Goddard Space Flight Center in **Greenbelt** is an exciting place to work. Goddard is an important part of the NASA science program. From high-tech control rooms, engineers operate spacecraft that conduct scientific experiments and explore the solar system.

Goddard's scientists also help us learn about our planet. They use technology to study changes in Earth's environment from space.

At Goddard's Wallops Flight Center, for example, sounding rockets, balloons, aircraft, and space shuttle carriers are launched into space. Then the equipment collects data and performs experiments to tell us about global climate changes.

The Goddard Space Flight Center is one of many technology programs that make Maryland a high-tech center. Thousands of other technology companies locate their businesses in Maryland because of its well-educated and well-trained workers.

Maryland is also a leading producer of electronic parts for computers. Marylanders build telecommunication systems that link people and information networks. They design and manufacture computer software programs used for business, government, scientific research, and medicine. Technology jobs are important to Maryland's future.

Other scientists in Maryland perform research to learn about the human body and medicine. The scientists study the body's cells through microscopes. They hope that what they learn will help them understand diseases better. Then they can look for ways to prevent or cure those diseases.

At the National Institutes of Health, researchers use technology to study human diseases from the common cold to rare illnesses. The researchers try to find out why we get sick, how we can get better when we are sick, and how we can prevent getting sick at all.

Maryland's Johns Hopkins University and School of Medicine also carries out high-tech research projects that search for cures for deadly diseases such as AIDS. Scientists in Maryland are learning from their research, and what they learn may help people all over the world.

REVIEW What makes Maryland one of the high-tech centers of the nation? Main Idea and Details

FACT FILE

Careers in Technology and Government

The federal government employs Marylanders to run government programs and solve some of the nation's most important problems. Marylanders work in high-tech jobs that provide government security, food safety, ocean research, and space exploration.

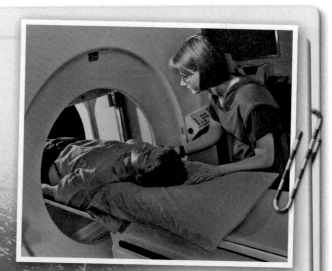

▶ Marylanders have careers in many kinds of medical research that help people live healthier, more productive lives.

▶ Students in Bethesda, Maryland, are learning to use high-tech equipment as they prepare for future careers.

▶ Careers in space and deep ocean research add to our understanding of Earth.

35

Working for the Federal Government

You have read about the exciting jobs at the Goddard Space Flight Center. Goddard's workers are employees of the federal government. The people of our country pay them to do important research jobs. Many other Marylanders have government jobs in nearby Washington, D.C.

Some Marylanders work for federal agencies located within the state. The National Institutes of Health and the National Institute of Standards and Technology in Maryland provide jobs for thousands of people.

Workers at the Food and Drug Administration (FDA) in **Rockville** have important responsibilities. They make sure that the foods we eat and the products and medicines we use are safe and effective. Scientists, engineers, biologists, and other FDA workers test products, including medicines, to make sure that they are good enough to get an FDA seal of approval.

▶ **Many Marylanders commute from their homes to work in Washington, D.C., in many different federal government offices.**

Each morning many thousands of Marylanders commute along the 40-mile corridor between Baltimore, Maryland, and Washington, D.C. Many work in government agencies, museums, schools, hospitals, and military bases. More than 125,000 Marylanders work in federal government service jobs. Marylanders truly serve the nation.

Hundreds of federal agencies in Washington, D.C., take care of the nation's business. These agencies manage money, protect the nation, oversee schools, and protect the environment. Many Marylanders apply for job openings at these agencies each year.

The Social Security Administration manages money to provide income for older Americans after they retire from working. The Defense Department is charged with keeping our nation safe. The Department of Education hires people to oversee our nation's schools.

The Environmental Protection Agency (EPA) employs thousands of people to protect human health and Earth's environment. The EPA watches over our

▶ **Workers at the Smithsonian Institution's museums help care for and preserve our nation's treasures.**

nation's air, water, and land to keep them safe from pollution.

Many Marylanders work for the Smithsonian Institution in Washington, D.C. The Smithsonian museums collect and display our nation's treasures. At these museums Americans can see a wide variety of items from the nation's history in politics, science, television, and art.

Historians, exhibit designers, tour guides, educators, architects, secretaries, researchers, and artists are just some of the jobs at the Smithsonian. All of these workers serve the millions of people who visit the exhibits and participate in educational programs at one of the world's most impressive museums.

Federal Government Employees, 2001	
State	**Number of People Employed in Federal Government**
Delaware	5,600
Maryland	126,782
Pennsylvania	105,900
Virginia	150,400
West Virginia	21,807

▶ **Like other states near Washington, D.C., Maryland sends thousands of workers to perform jobs in the federal government.**

REVIEW How are working at the Goddard Space Center and at the Smithsonian alike and different? Compare and Contrast

Welcoming Tourists

About 18 million tourists come each year to enjoy Maryland's many attractions. To make their stay a pleasant one, more than 100,000 workers have jobs in tourism. That makes tourism Maryland's fourth-largest employer.

You have read that Maryland has been called America in miniature because of the great variety of its landforms, cultures, and attractions. That variety attracts visitors from all over. Some come to ski, sail, fish, hike, or sunbathe on Maryland beaches. Others visit Antietam and other historical Civil War battle sites. In Baltimore many visitors enjoy the Inner Harbor area and the National Aquarium.

In the western mountains, tourism is related to the region's history and its natural beauty. Some Marylanders serve as museum guides at the B&O Railroad Museum. Others teach rock climbing, lead nature hikes, and manage hotels for visiting fishers and bicyclists.

At the Wisp Mountain Resort, winter tourists enjoy skiing and snowboarding with the help of local instructors. Many behind-the-scenes workers help make the experience fun. Restaurant staff members, hotel workers, equipment rental shop clerks, and a variety of other guest service workers are all part of Maryland's tourist industries.

▶ Skiing and snowboarding are popular winter sports at Wisp Mountain's ski runs.

Maryland's farmers also enjoy the additional income from tourism. As part of organized tours, Marylanders welcome visitors to their farms and dairies for hands-on experiences and educational programs.

Each year thousands of people attend Maryland's Preakness® Stakes, one of horse racing's most important events. Trainers on Maryland's thoroughbred horse farms help prepare horses for the big race.

Maryland's Eastern Shore leads the state in income from tourism. Resort towns such as Ocean City employ hundreds of people. Picture having a job helping people learn to fly kites at Maryland's International Kite Exposition!

Tourists in Ocean City can get close to nature too. They can deep-sea fish for marlin or take an eco-cruise to see dolphins and whales off the coast.

The Ocean City Convention Center employs people to host events that bring

▶ Hundreds of service workers in Ocean City provide tourists with food and lodging.

▶ Maryland's horse trainers prepare thoroughbred horses to compete in races.

visitors to festivals, concerts, and antique shows. More than half of the people who live in Worcester County, which includes Ocean City, work in jobs related to tourism.

In other parts of the Eastern Shore, tourists come to see skipjack races and take boat rides to Smith Island or Tilghman Island. Restaurants in the area serve famous oyster and crab dishes prepared by Maryland chefs. Local fishers help tourists try their hand at crabbing.

Eastern Shore nature guides introduce tourists to the Blackwater National Wildlife Refuge and its wildlife. Maryland's great variety supplies many jobs for its people.

REVIEW Write a summary of the kinds of jobs Marylanders do to welcome visitors to their state. ⟳ Summarize

Harvesting Resources

You have read about Maryland's farms, forests, and waterways. Many Marylanders earn salaries from activities related to farming or mining.

About one-third of Maryland's land is used for agriculture. In addition to the farm crops, fruits, vegetables, and animals that Maryland farmers raise, farms also create jobs for many other Marylanders. In all, more than 67,000 people in Maryland make their living from agricultural work, mostly in the north central or upper Eastern Shore areas. Income from farming is more than $5 billion each year.

Marylanders who work for the Department of Agriculture have jobs that help support Maryland's farmers as they work with their crops and animals. For example, Department of Agriculture workers may look for ways to help cows produce better milk—and more of it!

▶ Maryland has more than 12,000 farms.

The milk may be shipped to an ice cream maker, who then sells the finished ice cream to an ice cream shop. The ice cream may finally end up in the ice cream soda that you enjoy after an afternoon at the beach.

If a farmer grows soybeans, his products may end up in baby formula or printer's ink for newspapers. All the people who manufacture and sell these products have jobs based on agriculture and Maryland's resources.

In western Maryland, some people earn a living from the state's minerals.

▶ In the summer Maryland farmers harvest sweetcorn for people to eat. In the fall they harvest fieldcorn for animal food and other uses.

Harvesting Maryland's Resources

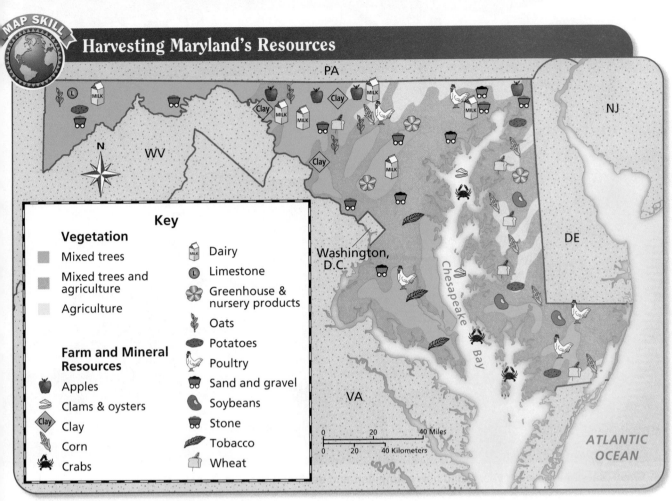

Key

Vegetation

- Mixed trees
- Mixed trees and agriculture
- Agriculture

Farm and Mineral Resources

- 🍎 Apples
- Clams & oysters
- Clay Clay
- Corn
- 🦀 Crabs
- 🥛 Dairy
- Ⓛ Limestone
- Greenhouse & nursery products
- Oats
- Potatoes
- Poultry
- Sand and gravel
- Soybeans
- Stone
- Tobacco
- Wheat

▶ **Land and water provide Marylanders with a variety of resources.**

MAP SKILL Use a Map Key *Where is seafood an important resource?*

They mine coal, marble, and limestone in the more than 90 mines located in the state's mountains. Harford County, for example, produces sand, gravel, and clay in the plains area and granite material and crushed stone in the plateau area of the county. Quarries that once produced slate and green marble can still be found in the Whiteford-Cardiff area. Like agricultural products, the marble and limestone create other jobs as they are processed, sold, and used in building projects.

REVIEW Summarize the kinds of products produced from Maryland's land resources. ↻ **Summarize**

▶ **Raising broilers brings a large share of farm income to Maryland.**

▶ **Many Marylanders work year-round harvesting fish and seafood from Chesapeake Bay.**

Maryland's Water Resources

One of Maryland's richest resources is Chesapeake Bay and its tributaries. Many Marylanders find jobs related to harvesting the bay's rich seafood. Water resources contribute to Maryland's economy in two ways. The waterways support commercial fishers and sport fishers.

Commercial fishers harvested more than $60 million worth of seafood in 1995. Commercial fishing helped the economies of many communities in Maryland, such as Baltimore, Ocean City, St. Michaels, Tilghman Island, Cambridge, Easton, Chesterton, Aberdeen, Pocomoke City, Annapolis, and Solomons.

Commerical fishers can harvest blue crabs most of the year. In the fall, they begin harvesting oysters. They also fish for striped bass, perch, eel, catfish, yellow perch, and soft-shell crabs.

Part of that income, though, does not come from commercial fishing, or fishing as a business. Instead, people who fish for fun and sport come to Maryland for freshwater and saltwater fishing. A government source says that more than 430,000 sport fishers from around the world fish in Maryland waters. Their activities bring hundreds of millions of dollars to Maryland's economy. In fact, the sales taxes that Maryland's sport fishers pay may help support the school you attend and the roads you used to get there.

Anglers, or sport fishers, pay more than $20 million in Maryland sales tax each year.

Only a little more than one-third of Maryland's sport fishing is in the saltwater of the bay and the ocean. The rest is in Maryland's rivers and lakes.

Although sport anglers fish for fun, many people benefit from their activities. About 5,000 people in cities and towns such as Baltimore and Ocean City have jobs that provide products and services to sport fishers. Some sell fishing equipment. Others sell bait or rent fishing boats. Some provide charter services that take fishers into the bay or ocean.

In the 1980s Maryland was in danger of losing this important resource. About 70 percent of Maryland's wetlands had already been lost. Wetlands are important to the fishing economy. These areas are nurseries for young fish and provide food for many species.

▶ Commercial fishers are important to Maryland's economy.

▶ Maryland's chefs prepare seafood for Marylanders and visitors.

Many of Maryland's communities began working with the federal government to save Chesapeake Bay and to protect the wetlands. Though it will take a long time to undo the damage to the wetlands and the bay, Marylanders are making progress in protecting their important fishing industry.

REVIEW Summarize the ways that Maryland's water resources contribute to the state's fishing economy.
🔄 Summarize

Shipping and Manufacturing

The bay also provides jobs in shipping and manufacturing. The Army Corps of Engineers reports that 27,000 ships were handled in Baltimore's Harbor in 1999. Workers load ships and send off coal, corn, soybeans, and other Maryland products. They unload cars, trucks, iron ore, fertilizer, and sugar. Tugboat captains guide the big ships safely in and out of the port.

Maryland's **longshoremen,** the port workers who load and unload ships, can handle any cargo, any time, in any weather. The port is open 24 hours a day to handle shipping jobs. The crane operators are skilled in operating the huge, powerful equipment that lifts tons of cargo containers.

In Baltimore's World Trade Center, Marylanders work for the Maryland Port Administration and for the shipping companies that have headquarters there. Cruise ship companies that take vacationers from Baltimore's harbor to ports around the world hire Marylanders for their ships and offices.

▶ **Maryland's longshoremen handle tons of cargo in the Baltimore port.**

Many of the products shipped out of Baltimore's port are manufactured in Maryland. Manufacturing employs about one of every fifteen workers in the state. Maryland's cannery workers clean, cook, and can fish and other seafood before it is shipped around the world. Maryland's good transportation systems make it easy and profitable to share the products with the rest of the country and the world.

Maryland has been an important manufacturing center since colonial times. Many Marylanders continue to earn their living by making products.

▶ **Seafood processing is an important source of income for Maryland.**

44

Shipbuilding companies along Chesapeake Bay make boats for different kinds of activities. From small skipjacks to motorboats and huge cargo ships, shipbuilding is a Maryland tradition. Some of Maryland's skilled shipbuilders work for the Department of Defense, building and repairing navy ships.

Maryland's manufacturing jobs require high levels of technical skills. The state's products are as varied as its resources. The largest industries in the state employ people to make chemicals, soap, cleaning products, computer products, and hardware. Other Marylanders produce satellite communication equipment, spices, and shoes.

Together, Marylanders produce more than $36 billion worth of products each year. These products are sold to people in the state, the rest of the United States, and countries all over the world.

REVIEW What products do Maryland companies manufacture? Main Idea and Details

Summarize the Lesson

- Maryland's economy benefits from its location and diverse resources.
- At Goddard Space Flight Center and other high-tech companies, Marylanders use their technological skills.
- Many Marylanders work for the federal government.
- Welcoming tourists creates many jobs for Marylanders.
- Marylanders harvest their state's resources through farming, fishing, and mining.
- The busy port of Baltimore ships many products manufactured in Maryland.

LESSON 4　REVIEW

Check Facts and Main Ideas

1. ↻ Summarize On a separate sheet of paper, draw the graphic organizer and fill in information that helps summarize the lesson.

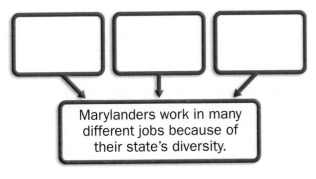

Marylanders work in many different jobs because of their state's diversity.

2. How do Marylanders use their technological skills in their work?
3. What kinds of jobs do Marylanders perform for the federal government?
4. How do Maryland's resources in different locations create jobs?
5. **Critical Thinking: *Cause and Effect*** Why is Baltimore one of the leading shipping and trading cities in the United States?

Link to ⬤⬤ Mathematics

Solve a Math Problem You have read on page 38 that 100,000 Marylanders work in the tourist industry and that 18 million tourists come to Maryland each year. Using division, find out about how many tourists each Marylander in tourism serves each year.

Chapter Summary

Summarize

Target Skill

On a separate sheet of paper, make a diagram like the one shown. Fill in information to help summarize the different kinds of activities available because of Maryland's geography.

Maryland's geography creates opportunities for many kinds of activities.

Main Ideas and Skills

1. **Main Idea** How many geographic regions are in Maryland? Name them.

2. **Main Idea** What are Maryland's most important waterways?

3. **Main Idea** What transportation and communication systems link Maryland to the world?

4. **Main Idea** How do natural resources provide jobs for people in Maryland?

5. **Critical Thinking:** *Compare and Contrast* How are land and resources different in Maryland's three regions?

Apply Skills

Read a Circle Graph Use the circle graph on page 28 to answer the question.

6. What activity produced the smallest share of Maryland's income from natural resources in 1999?

Vocabulary and Places

Match each word with the correct definition or description.

1. **swamp** (p. 9)
2. **estuary** (p. 10)
3. **piedmont** (p. 16)
4. **deforestation** (p. 26)
5. **longshoreman** (p. 44)

a. a coastal waterway in which river water and saltwater from the ocean mix

b. at the foot of a mountain

c. cutting down forests

d. port workers who load and unload ships

e. a watery area with trees

Write a sentence about each of the following places. You may use two or more in a single sentence.

6. Baltimore (p. 7)
7. Ocean City (p. 9)
8. Appalachian Mountains (p. 13)
9. Delmarva Peninsula (p. 14)
10. Crisfield (p. 21)

Write About Maryland

1. **Write a postcard** to a friend about the region of Maryland in which you live. Explain why it is an ideal place to live.

2. **Write a report** about the many different kinds of farm products produced in your state.

3. **Write an article** for your school newspaper about why it is important to protect Maryland's forests.

The History of
Maryland

CHAPTER 2

Lesson 1

St. Mary's City

Maryland's settlement began in prehistory and grew when Europeans and Africans arrived.

Lesson 2

Chester Town

Maryland fought for independence and donated land for the new nation's capital.

Lesson 3

Fort McHenry

When Americans fought the British a second time, Maryland helped the United States win the war.

Lesson 4

Antietam Creek

The issue of slavery divided Maryland's people during the Civil War.

Lesson 5

Baltimore

After the Civil War, Baltimore grew to become one of the largest cities in the United States.

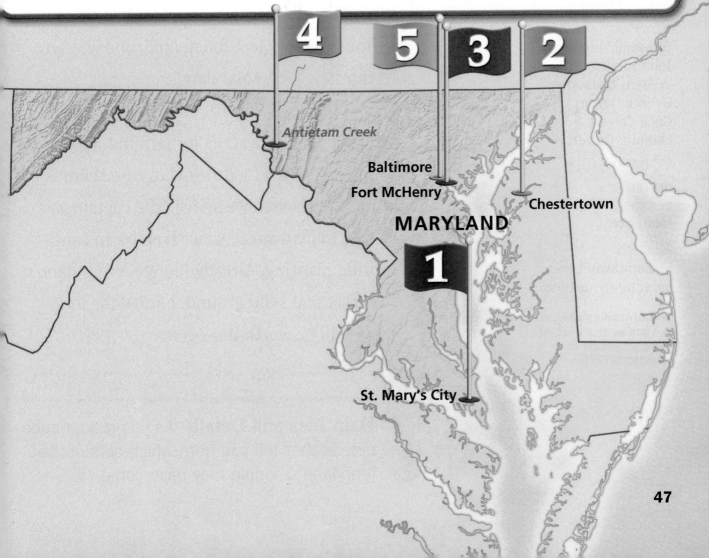

Antietam Creek

Baltimore

Fort McHenry

MARYLAND

Chestertown

St. Mary's City

1600			1700		1800

1608
John Smith explores the Chesapeake Bay.

1621
William Claiborne arrives in Chesapeake Bay.

1634
The *Ark* and the *Dove* arrive in Maryland.

1649
The Religious Tolerance Act is passed.

1767
The Mason-Dixon Line is set.

Maryland's Beginnings

St. Mary's City
St. Clement's Island
Chesapeake Bay

PREVIEW

Focus on the Main Idea
Maryland's early settlement began in prehistory and grew with the arrival of people from Europe and Africa.

PLACES
Chesapeake Bay
St. Clement's Island
St. Mary's City

PEOPLE
Giovanni Verrazano
John Smith
William Claiborne
George Calvert
Cecil Calvert
Leonard Calvert

VOCABULARY
artifact
persecution
tolerance

TERMS
Mason-Dixon Line
indentured servant

▶ Early sailors used devices such as this sextant to determine their location on the ocean.

You Are There

November 1633
Dear Diary,

Can it be that the ocean is finally calm? Last night's storm was so fierce that the mainsail came close to breaking! But this morning the *Ark* rocks gently. I look forward to the time when my feet touch land, and we can start our new life in Maryland!

The ship is packed with everything we need for the trip. We have seeds for farming, tools for working, and dried food stored in case there is nothing to eat when we arrive. The captain was very wise to plan ahead so we'll arrive in time for spring planting. Already I long for Maryland's green trees and solid ground. I know the long journey will be worth it!

Main Idea and Details As you read, notice details that tell you from which continents Maryland's people may have come.

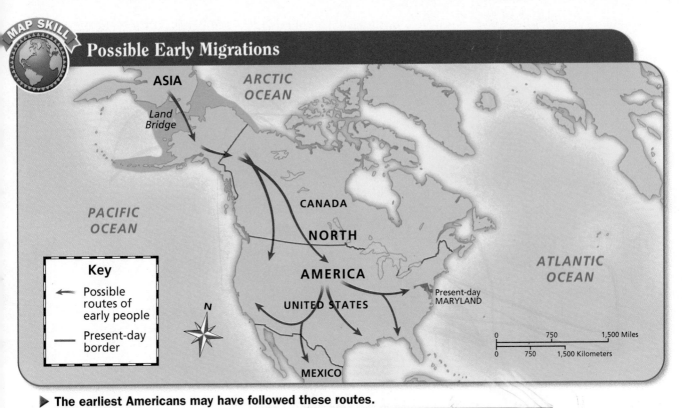

MAP SKILL

Possible Early Migrations

ASIA

ARCTIC OCEAN

Land Bridge

PACIFIC OCEAN

CANADA

NORTH

AMERICA

ATLANTIC OCEAN

UNITED STATES

Present-day MARYLAND

N

MEXICO

Key

← Possible routes of early people

— Present-day border

0   750   1,500 Miles
0   750   1,500 Kilometers

▶ The earliest Americans may have followed these routes.

MAP SKILL Use a Map Key *Trace the path that early people may have followed to reach the land now known as Maryland. In what present-day nations might they have passed?*

People Arrive

Long ago, icy glaciers covered the area that is now Maryland, so no one could live there. Many scientists believe that the area's first people arrived about 10,000 years ago in a time called prehistory. During prehistory, there was no system of writing, so we know little about these people's lives.

Scientists have found stone spear points and other artifacts that help tell us about people's lives. An artifact is anything made by human skill or work. These people moved from place to place, hunting, fishing, and gathering nuts.

As glacier ice melted, water filled the seas and flooded some of the land.

When the Susquehanna River flooded, Chesapeake Bay was born. The bay and new rivers changed people's lives.

The land around the bay was fertile, and fish were plentiful, so people did not need to keep moving from place to place. They built homes and small villages. They learned to plant seeds. In time corn, beans, and squash became important crops. They also made pots and tools.

Soon early people learned to store food. Stored food allowed them to stay in one location. As they learned better ways to store food, their villages became larger. Many different communities began to form in Maryland. Each had its own leaders and protected its land and way of life.

REVIEW Summarize the changes that allowed Maryland's first people to stay in one place. ⟲ **Summarize**

▶ Maryland's first people made stone tools such as this axe head.

49

▶ The Piscataway and other Native Americans in the land that we now call Maryland built villages and learned to harvest resources.

Maryland's Native American Cultures

You have read that early people changed from wanderers to village dwellers. When Europeans arrived, there may have been several thousand Native Americans living in villages in the area now known as Maryland.

People did different jobs in their communities. The men hunted. They fished with nets and spears from canoes made from tree trunks. The women grew corn, beans, and squash. Children worked too, gathering clams, oysters, and berries.

People built small houses covered with bark or grass mats. Sometimes these houses are called wigwams or lodges.

People in each of the settlements spoke a form of the Algonquian language. They understood each other and were able to trade food and other supplies with neighboring villages.

By the 1600s many different Native American groups called the land that is now Maryland their home. Many of Maryland's rivers and towns are named for these Native Americans, such as the Susquehanna River and the city of Piscataway.

The Nanticoke or "Tidewater People," lived on the eastern shore of Chesapeake Bay. Their land was marshy and not very good for farming. Instead of growing crops, most Nanticoke hunted and fished.

▶ Artifacts teach us about early Native American cultures. These pottery pieces were dug up in Annapolis' old town and reassembled.

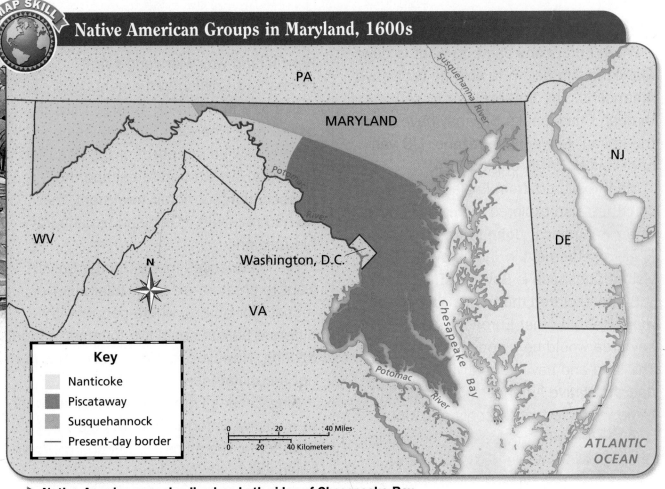

Native American Groups in Maryland, 1600s

PA

MARYLAND

NJ

Susquehanna River

Potomac River

WV

Washington, D.C.

DE

N

VA

Chesapeake Bay

Key

- Nanticoke
- Piscataway
- Susquehannock
- Present-day border

Potomac River

0   20   40 Miles
0   20   40 Kilometers

ATLANTIC OCEAN

▶ Native American peoples lived on both sides of Chesapeake Bay.

MAP SKILL Use a Map Key *Where were the Piscataway and Nanticoke people located?*

The Nanticoke also made beautiful beads from the clam shells they gathered. Then they traded the beads to groups that lived farther from the bay for things they needed but could not find near their homes.

The Piscataway people lived peacefully in the Potomac River valley. They farmed, fished, and hunted. Men and women had separate jobs. Men used spears and traps to catch fish, turtles, and eels. Piscataway women farmed and cooked. Sometimes they made stews of meat and fish or a corn dish called hominy. In some villages women as well as men became community leaders.

The Piscataway wore only a few light-weight clothes in the summer but kept warm with furs in the winter. Both men and women wore jewelry made from shells.

To the north lived the Susquehannock people. Sometimes the Susquehannock, a large Native American group in Maryland, fought battles with their southern neighbors to gain lands and goods.

REVIEW In what ways were the Nanticoke and Piscataway peoples alike? In what ways were they different? **Compare and Contrast**

European Settlers Arrive

When Europeans came to what is now Maryland, life began to change for Native Americans. The first explorer to sail through Chesapeake Bay may have been the Italian **Giovanni Verrazano** (JO van nee vair ah ZAHN oh) in 1524.

Many explorers from England and other countries also explored the eastern coast of North America. **John Smith** from the English settlement in Jamestown, Virginia, visited Chesapeake Bay in 1608.

Smith explored the area and made a map. He told other Europeans that the bay area would be a good place to settle. The land and bay had many resources, and the Native Americans were willing to trade valuable furs for tools and cloth.

In 1621 **William Claiborne** arrived in Chesapeake Bay. He settled on Kent Island, which he bought from the Native American people. The trading post on Kent Island was Maryland's first permanent English settlement.

In 1629 in England, **George Calvert** asked King Charles I for permission to start a new colony north of the Potomac River. Calvert wanted to escape the **persecution,** or unfair treatment, that he had received in England because of his religion.

His experiences made George Calvert want to create a place of **tolerance,** or respect for others, where people with different beliefs could live together without fighting. However, religious freedom was not a popular idea at this time.

King Charles I granted permission for the new colony. Unfortunately, George Calvert died before the ships the *Ark* and the *Dove* could sail to the new land.

▶ Calvert's ships, the *Ark* and the *Dove*, set out from England to start the Maryland colony.

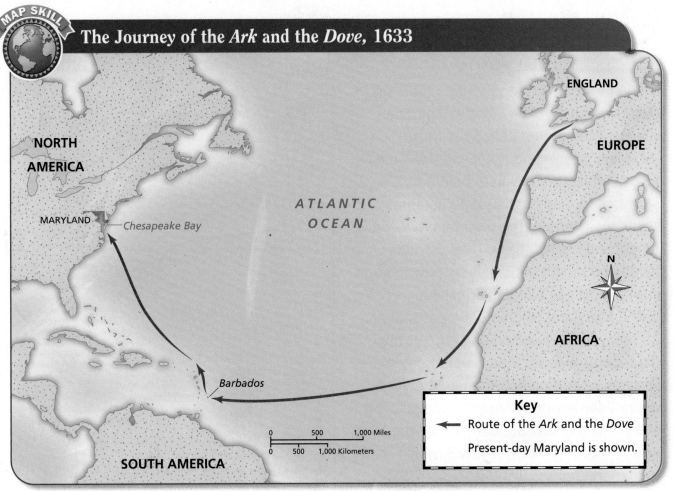

MAP SKILL

The Journey of the *Ark* and the *Dove*, 1633

ENGLAND

EUROPE

NORTH AMERICA

ATLANTIC OCEAN

MARYLAND — Chesapeake Bay

N

AFRICA

Barbados

0   500   1,000 Miles
0   500   1,000 Kilometers

SOUTH AMERICA

Key
← Route of the *Ark* and the *Dove*
Present-day Maryland is shown.

▶ The *Ark* and the *Dove* sailed across the Atlantic Ocean to bring colonists to Maryland.

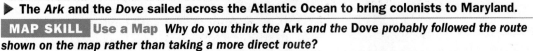

MAP SKILL Use a Map *Why do you think the Ark and the Dove probably followed the route shown on the map rather than taking a more direct route?*

His son **Cecil Calvert** inherited the rights to the Maryland colony. The colony was named Maryland after the wife of King Charles I. Her name was Henrietta Maria. Most of the people who signed up for the journey to the colony were farmers or skilled workers ready for jobs in the new settlement. Some were Catholic, and some were Protestants. Many hoped for a new start and a better life.

About 150 people set sail in the fall of 1633. **Leonard Calvert,** George Calvert's other son, led the journey. Cecil Calvert stayed in England to make sure no one tried to steal the Calvert claim to the colony.

The voyage was dangerous and long. During the voyage a storm separated the boats, but they found each other again at the island of Barbados in the Caribbean Sea. As the map shows, the *Ark* and the *Dove* continued from Barbados to Maryland and the Potomac River area. When they reached **St. Clement's Island,** the weary voyagers held a thanksgiving ceremony to celebrate their safe arrival in their new homeland.

REVIEW Summarize the reasons that people signed up for the voyage to Maryland. ⟳ Summarize

Life in Colonial Maryland

Leonard Calvert traded metal tools and cloth in exchange for a Native American village. The settlers called their town St. Mary's City, and it became Maryland's first capital. The colonists built a fort, a storehouse, and English-style homes.

Life was hard for the colonists, but Native Americans helped them. They provided fields and taught the colonists how to plant corn and to use canoes for fishing.

The Maryland colonists did not starve as many in some colonies had, but they did face problems. Many caught diseases. Dreams of getting rich from gold and silver did not come true for most colonists. But Maryland had one big attraction—the land was good for growing tobacco, which the people in England wanted.

New people continued to come to Maryland because of its religious freedom. The Calvert family helped pass the Religious Toleration Act in 1649. But the religious freedom did not last long. The Calvert family finally lost control of the colony in 1689, when the English king and queen, William III and Mary II, claimed it.

Then Maryland and Pennsylvania fought for control over land borders. The two colonies could not agree on their borders and both claimed the same land. In 1763 Charles Mason and Jeremiah Dixon came from England to set the boundary line.

After four long years, they established the 233-mile **Mason-Dixon Line** to divide the land fairly. Today the Mason-Dixon Line is viewed as the border between Northern and Southern states.

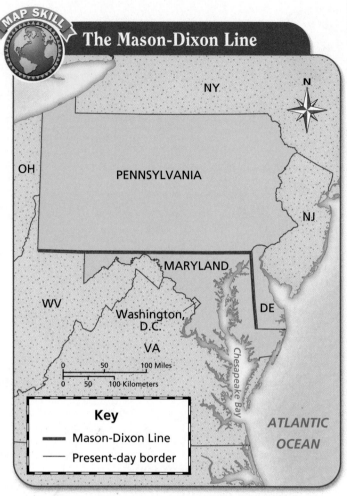

The Mason-Dixon Line

MAP SKILL

Key
— Mason-Dixon Line
— Present-day border

▶ Charles Mason and Jeremiah Dixon spent four years surveying to set Maryland's borders.

MAP SKILL Read a Map *About how long is the Mason-Dixon Line?*

▶ After colonists settled in St. Mary's City, new towns such as Baltimore and Annapolis were founded.

You have read that the colonists and the Native Americans helped each other. They traded goods and information that made life better for all. But more colonists arrived and wanted land for crops such as tobacco. Native Americans were soon pushed off of their land, often into areas where other groups lived. Some fought unsuccessfully to keep their lands. Many became sick and died from diseases brought by the Europeans. In time, few Native Americans were left in Maryland.

REVIEW Explain how colonists and Native Americans got along when the colony first began and then later on. **Compare and Contrast**

FACT FILE

St. Mary's Colonial Village

In St. Mary's village, visitors can see colonial activities carried out by modern people in authentic-style costumes.

▶ Many colonial supplies had to be shipped to St. Mary's City from England, as this re-creation shows.

▶ Colonists raised their own food as this costumed actor shows.

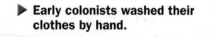

▶ Early colonists washed their clothes by hand.

55

Working in Colonial Maryland

Many of Maryland's settlers signed contracts to work for others. These **indentured servants,** or contract laborers, agreed to give labor to the person who paid for their voyage from Europe. After several years indentured servants were free to buy their own land or to work in jobs of their choice with pay.

▶ **Tobacco fields demanded large numbers of workers.**

Many indentured servants continued to work on tobacco plantations. But as the plantations grew larger, even more workers were needed. People were taken from Africa and forced to work on these large plantations without being paid. These workers were enslaved and did not come to America freely. Many of them were treated badly by plantation owners.

REVIEW Briefly summarize how plantation owners solved the problem of getting workers. ↻ Summarize

Summarize the Lesson

- **1608** John Smith explored the Chesapeake Bay.
- **1631** William Claiborne arrived in Chesapeake Bay.
- **1634** The *Ark* and the *Dove* arrived.
- **1649** The Religious Tolerance Act was passed.
- **1767** The Mason-Dixon Line was set.

LESSON 1 REVIEW

Check Facts and Main Ideas

1. **Main Idea and Details** On a separate sheet of paper, fill in the diagram to show from which continents the people of what is now Maryland might have come.

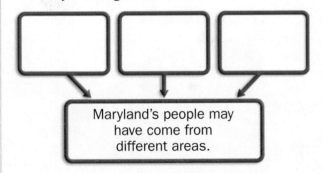

Maryland's people may have come from different areas.

2. What is known about the people who lived in what is now Maryland before the Europeans arrived?

3. Why did people from Europe come to settle in the colony of Maryland?

4. What hardships did colonists face, and how did they overcome them?

5. **Critical Thinking:** *Cause and Effect* Why were Africans enslaved in Maryland?

Link to ∞ Art

Make a Drawing Create your own drawing of a scene from the Maryland colony. Think about all of the different things people did to stay alive and build the colony.

George Calvert, First Baron Baltimore

1580–1632

George Calvert grew up in Yorkshire in northern England. He went to Oxford University and became a political leader. He was later hired to become a secretary for Sir Robert Cecil, the king's minister.

Calvert impressed King James I. The king knighted him in 1617 and appointed him secretary of state in 1619. He served in Parliament, and King James I (and later King Charles I) rewarded him with grants of land and money.

In 1625 Calvert made a religious decision that changed his life. He became a Roman Catholic in a country that believed in only one church, the Protestant Church of England. Calvert resigned his government job. The king made him First Baron Baltimore and gave him a large estate in Ireland.

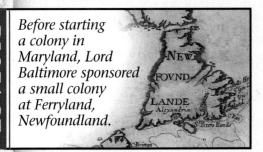

BIOFACT

Before starting a colony in Maryland, Lord Baltimore sponsored a small colony at Ferryland, Newfoundland.

But Calvert dreamed of a place where people could have religious freedom. He asked the king for a grant of land near the Potomac River in North America. Finally an agreement was prepared, but—sadly—Calvert died before he could sail to Maryland. His son, Cecil, signed people up for the voyage and his son, Leonard, led the colonists to Maryland.

Learn from Biographies

Why did George Calvert want to start a colony in Maryland?

Students can research the lives of significant people by clicking on *Meet the People* at **www.sfsocialstudies.com**.

1775	1780	1785	1790

1775
The American Revolution begins.

1784
The Treaty of Paris is approved.

1788
Maryland becomes the seventh state.

1791
Maryland donates land for Washington, D.C.

MARYLAND

Chester Town•
Annapolis•

Maryland Fights for Freedom

PREVIEW

Focus on the Main Idea
Maryland fought for independence and shared land with the nation.

PLACES
Chester Town
Annapolis

PEOPLE
Anthony Stewart
Samuel Chase
William Paca
Thomas Stone
Charles Carroll
John Hanson

VOCABULARY
privateer

TERMS
Stamp Act
Townshend Acts
First Continental Congress
Second Continental Congress
Treaty of Paris

EVENTS
Chester Town Tea Party
Battle of Long Island

You Are There

May 1774

"Oh! Look at all that tea!" you say to your little brother. He holds your hand tightly as he leans over the edge of the pier with you, looking down into the murky water of the Chester River.

"Why did those people dump the tea in there?" he asks you, pointing at the water.

"The British want us to pay taxes on tea. They want us to pay taxes on a lot of things. And they want us to follow their laws," you explain.

Your little brother scrunches up his face.

"I think we should make our own laws," he tells you as he stomps his foot.

"That's what the people who dumped the tea also thought!" you declare.

Main Idea and Details As you read, look for details that explain how Maryland became independent.

The Road to Revolution

You have read that Maryland was a colony. For many years, Great Britain and its colonies in America were on peaceful terms.

Things changed after Britain fought and won a war with France—the French and Indian War. The war was fought in America and cost a lot of money, so Britain needed money to pay its war debts.

British leaders thought that the colonies should help pay the debt because Britain protected the colonies. The **Stamp Act,** passed in 1765, required colonists to buy special stamps for newspapers and legal papers. In 1767 Britain passed the **Townshend Acts,** which placed a tax on glass, paint, paper, and tea.

The two acts angered the colonists, because they could not vote for members of the British Parliament who passed the acts. Colonists stopped buying British goods and refused to pay the taxes. In **Chester Town,** some colonists held the

▶ Tax stamps like this one were required on all legal documents.

Chester Town Tea Party in 1774. They dumped a ship's cargo of tea into the river.

In Annapolis the *Peggy Stewart,* a ship owned by merchant **Anthony Stewart,** sailed into the harbor carrying 2,300 pounds of tea. Angry colonists threatened Stewart. They frightened him so much that he apologized for having the tea and set fire to his own ship and its cargo!

Tensions between Britain and the colonies continued to grow. Representatives from the colonies, including some Marylanders, met and formed the **First Continental Congress.** They wrote letters to Britain asking for an end to the taxes. The representatives warned all of the colonists that war with Britain might be necessary if Britain did not agree.

REVIEW Briefly summarize how some colonists reacted to British taxes.
↺ **Summarize**

▶ The people of Chester Town (now known as Chestertown) dumped tea into the river to protest Britain's tax on tea, as this reenactment shows.

The Old Line State

People from Maryland and other colonies understood that war might be coming. They began to take sides. Some wanted their independence. They wanted the right to make their own laws, and they did not want to pay taxes passed by people whom they did not elect. Others thought that the colonies should stay loyal to Britain.

In 1775 the Second Continental Congress met and tried again to solve the colonies' problems with Britain peacefully. But Britain did not wish to lessen its control of the colonies.

Colonists and British soldiers began to fight in other colonies. Maryland and the other colonies decided to prepare for war with Britain. The American Revolution had begun. No major battles were fought in Maryland during the American Revolution, but Maryland played an important role in winning independence from Britain, which you will read about later.

In 1776 the Second Continental Congress continued to meet. While the war was being fought, the Congress, including Marylanders Samuel Chase, William Paca, Thomas Stone, and Charles Carroll, signed the Declaration of Independence.

▶ The Second Continental Congress passed the Declaration of Independence. Four Marylanders signed the historic document.

These four Marylanders continued to fight for rights and independence after signing the Declaration. Chase and Paca served as state judges. Paca also served as governor and chief justice. After serving another term in Congress, Stone retired. Carroll helped form Maryland's government and write its constitution. He served in the U.S. Senate from 1789–1792.

In 1781 Marylander **John Hanson** was elected by Congress as the first president of the Congress of the Confederacy before the Constitution was written. Marylanders played an important role in our nation's early government.

On the battlefield, Maryland's soldiers were known for their bravery. Maryland was one of the first colonies to recruit troops for the new Continental Army. About 23,000 soldiers from Maryland traveled to the other colonies to fight in battles.

General George Washington often gave Maryland troops the most dangerous jobs. In the **Battle of Long Island** in New York, Marylanders protected Washington's troops as they retreated in defeat. Washington called them "the troops of the line." Some historians say that is why Maryland is called "The Old Line State."

Although the soldiers were brave, war with Britain was difficult, especially at sea. Britain had a large navy with many warships. The colonies had a much smaller navy with few ships.

▶ **Privateers helped defeat the British Navy by stopping ships and seizing the cargo.**

The new government asked Marylanders and other colonists to use their own ships to help fight the war at sea. Many **privateers,** or citizens who owned armed ships, captured British ships and took their cargo. Baltimore harbor was home to many privateers. The Baltimore privateers became famous for their success at capturing and sinking ships.

The Battle of Yorktown was the final major battle of the war and an American victory. In 1781 General Washington sent Colonel Tench Tilghman, his aide from Maryland, to spread the news that the colonies had defeated Britain. Marylanders celebrated by firing 13 cannon rounds to honor each colony in the new United States of America. After six years, the war was finally ending.

REVIEW What were some of the contributions that Marylanders made in the Revolutionary War? **Main Idea and Details**

Maryland Contributes to the New Nation

By the end of the war, Maryland had become an important member of a new nation. **Annapolis** was named the nation's new capital city during our country's first year as the United States of America. In 1784 Congress met at Maryland's State House in Annapolis to approve the **Treaty of Paris.** This document finalized the peace agreement between Great Britain and the United States.

The new nation needed a new constitution. Five Marylanders went to Philadelphia to work with representatives from other states on creating this document. In the end, three Marylanders, James McHenry, Daniel Carroll, and Daniel of St. Thomas Jenifer signed the new Constitution of the United States of America.

Maryland's state convention met in 1788 to review the new U.S. Constitution. After several months of discussion, Maryland gave its approval and became the seventh state to join the United States. A few years later, Maryland lawmakers helped to adopt and approve the Bill of Rights.

The United States Naval Academy

The United States Navy was established during the Revolutionary War. In 1845 a naval school was established in Annapolis, Maryland. In 1850 the school became the United States Naval Academy.

▶ The Naval Academy started with 50 sailors in an old fort. The academy now trains thousands of students each year.

▶ Today both men and women attend the United States Naval Academy.

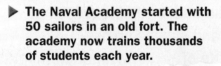

The new nation needed a permanent capital city. President Washington selected an area for the capital, which would not be a state but its own separate district. The land he selected included part of Maryland. Along with many other contributions to the new nation, Marylanders donated the land in 1791. In 1800 the government moved to a new capital city—Washington, D.C.

REVIEW In what ways did Maryland contribute to the new nation after the Revolutionary War ended?
Main Idea and Details

Summarize the Lesson

1775 The American Revolution began.

1784 The Treaty of Paris was approved.

1788 Maryland became the seventh state.

1791 Maryland donated land for Washington, D.C.

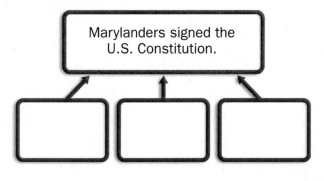

▶ The Revolutionary War ended when the United States and Britain signed the Treaty of Paris.

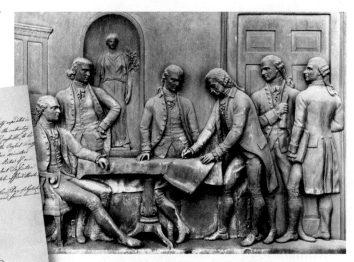

▶ The Treaty of Paris was signed in Paris, France. It was later approved in Annapolis, Maryland, in 1784.

LESSON 2   REVIEW

Check Facts and Main Ideas

1. **Main Idea and Details** On a separate sheet of paper, fill in the diagram to identify the three Marylanders who signed the U.S. Constitution.

```
Marylanders signed the
U.S. Constitution.
```

2. What are two events that made the colonists angry with Great Britain?

3. In what ways did Marylanders help win the war for independence?

4. How did Marylanders help build the nation after the war?

5. **Critical Thinking: Draw Conclusions** Why did some colonists not want to join the fight for independence?

Link to Writing

Write a Newspaper Story Write a newspaper article about the burning of the *Peggy Stewart* or another event in Maryland as it might have been written during Revolutionary War times.

1812
The War of
1812 begins.

1813
The British
attack Havre
de Grace.

1814
Francis Scott Key
writes "Defense
of Fort McHenry."

MARYLAND

Havre de Grace
Baltimore
Fort McHenry
Washington,
D.C.

Chesapeake
Bay

PREVIEW

Focus on the Main Idea
Marylanders helped the United States win the War of 1812 and helped the country grow.

PLACES
Baltimore
Chesapeake Bay
Havre de Grace
Washington, D.C.
Fort McHenry

PEOPLE
George Cockburn
Francis Scott Key
Mary Pickersgill

VOCABULARY
blockade
impressment
militia
anthem

TERMS
Chesapeake Blockade
National Road
iron horse

EVENT
Battle of Baltimore

▶ Mary Pickersgill's flag is one of the most famous flags in American history.

War and Growth

You Are There

July 1813

Dear Sarah,

Greetings from Baltimore! I hope you are well. We are having an exciting summer. In my last letter, I told you about my neighbor, Mary Pickersgill. She earns money by making flags. She is truly a proud and patriotic American. The exciting news is that she has been asked by Commodore Joshua Barney to make two flags for Fort McHenry. She just finished one flag.

Yesterday I visited with her as she worked on the second flag. She'll be paid more than $400! It will be the largest battle flag ever made. When it's finished, it will fly above Fort McHenry so that everyone can see that we are a free and independent country!

Main Idea and Details As you read, look for details that help explain how Maryland was part of the War of 1812.

Tensions with Britain

After the Revolutionary War, the United States wanted to trade with other countries as an independent nation. U.S. traders no longer had to follow Britain's rules or pay British taxes. They could trade freely and make a good profit.

Baltimore, like other towns near the water, became an exciting and successful trading port because of its location on Chesapeake Bay. Ships carrying cargo could easily move in and out of the bay.

While Britain was fighting a war with France, Baltimore traders sailed out of port carrying goods to many places, including France. The British were not happy. They were losing trade money that the United States was now making. France, Britain's enemy, was receiving the supplies needed to have a strong army and navy.

Britain tried to stop U.S. traders. British ships set up a blockade, or the stopping of ships from entering a port, in Chesapeake Bay to control what went in and out of Baltimore's harbor. They stopped American trading ships and took the cargo.

The British also held the sailors that they found on board the trading ships. Impressments, or sailor kidnappings and forced military service, forced many U.S. sailors to join the British Navy.

The Chesapeake Blockade increased tensions between the two countries. In 1812 the United States once again declared war on Britain.

REVIEW Summarize the reasons that the United States declared war on Britain in 1812. ⟳ **Summarize**

▶ Baltimore's harbor made that city a successful trading port for the new nation.

Maryland Defends Its Land

During the War of 1812, Maryland and the other states were ready to fight to protect their right to trade. When the British troops attacked, Marylanders defended their towns.

In 1813 British Admiral **George Cockburn** and his troops entered Maryland and attacked the town of **Havre de Grace.** Though the **militia,** or army of citizens, tried to defend the town, the British stole the supplies that they needed and burned Havre de Grace.

Washington, D.C., the nation's new capital, was the next British target. United States President James Madison narrowly escaped when Admiral Cockburn and his troops set fires in the capital.

To win the war, though, Britain would have to stop Baltimore's successful trading business. In 1814 the British planned a new attack.

Baltimore's militia joined with the U.S. Army and Navy to defend the city. About 250 volunteers marched out to meet the British. The **Battle of Baltimore** had begun.

On September 13, 1814, British ships fired on Baltimore's **Fort McHenry.** The battle went on throughout the night.

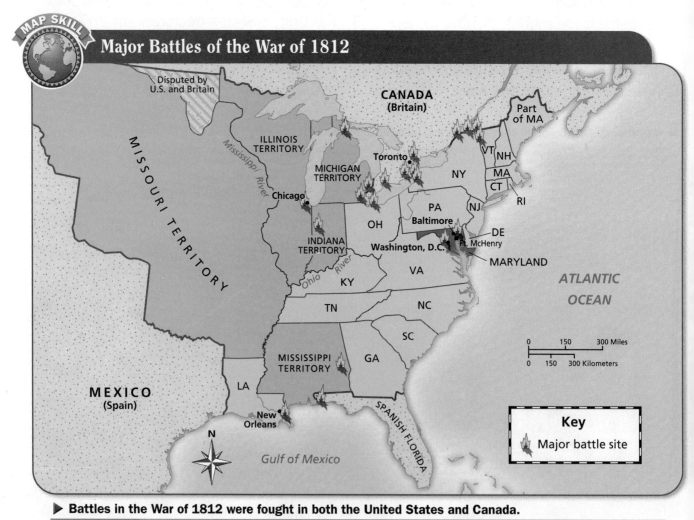

MAP SKILL

Major Battles of the War of 1812

Disputed by U.S. and Britain

CANADA (Britain)

Part of MA

ILLINOIS TERRITORY

Toronto

MISSOURI TERRITORY

MICHIGAN TERRITORY

Chicago

Mississippi River

VT NH

NY MA CT

RI

PA NJ

Baltimore

OH

DE

INDIANA TERRITORY

Washington, D.C.

Ft. McHenry

Ohio River

VA

MARYLAND

KY

ATLANTIC OCEAN

TN

NC

SC

MISSISSIPPI TERRITORY

GA

MEXICO (Spain)

LA

New Orleans

SPANISH FLORIDA

Gulf of Mexico

0   150   300 Miles
0   150   300 Kilometers

Key
Major battle site

▶ Battles in the War of 1812 were fought in both the United States and Canada.

MAP SKILL Use a Map Key *How many major battles in the War of 1812 were fought in Maryland?*

▶ The United States fought and won the Battle of Baltimore at Fort McHenry.

Francis Scott Key, a Maryland lawyer, watched the battle from a British ship. He had boarded the ship to try to win the release of a prisoner, but the British kept both men on board. Watching the 25-hour attack, Key wondered if the fort could survive.

At dawn the fighting stopped. Francis Scott Key was relieved to see the United States flag made by Mary Pickersgill still flying over Fort McHenry. The United States had won the Battle of Baltimore. Shortly after their defeat, the British agreed to end the war.

Francis Scott Key decided that such a victory called for a new poem. He wrote the poem that became our national anthem, or song of praise.

REVIEW Why was the Battle of Baltimore important in the War of 1812?
Main Idea and Details

Defense of Fort McHenry
by *Francis Scott Key*

Francis Scott Key's poem, "Defense of Fort McHenry," became "The Star-Spangled Banner" when it was set to music.

....

*Oh, say can you see, by the
dawn's early light,
What so proudly we hailed at the
twilight's last gleaming?
Whose broad stripes and bright
stars, through the perilous fight,
O'er the ramparts we watched,
were so gallantly streaming?
And the rockets' red glare, the
bombs bursting in air,
Gave proof through the night that
our flag was still there.
O say, does that star-spangled
banner yet wave
O'er the land of the free and the
home of the brave?*

New Ways to Travel

The period after the war was a time of great growth for Maryland. Baltimore was already a center for shipping and trade, but now many other forms of transportation were developing all over Maryland.

People wanted a better way to travel east from the Allegheny Mountains to Baltimore, and west over the mountains to the rich farmland of the Ohio Valley. The **National Road** became the first federally funded highway in the United States. It took the place of trails and footpaths that were difficult to navigate in bad weather.

The first stretch of road connected Cumberland, Maryland, to Wheeling, Virginia. Construction started at Cumberland in 1811 and reached Wheeling in 1818. Today, Wheeling is in West Virginia. By the 1830s the National Road stretched all the way from Maryland to Illinois.

Thousands of people traveled on the National Road to new homes in the west. During the busiest times, a steady stream of wagons, coaches, and horseback riders shared the road. National Road cities such as Cumberland began to grow, and businesses offering places to sleep and eat opened along the route.

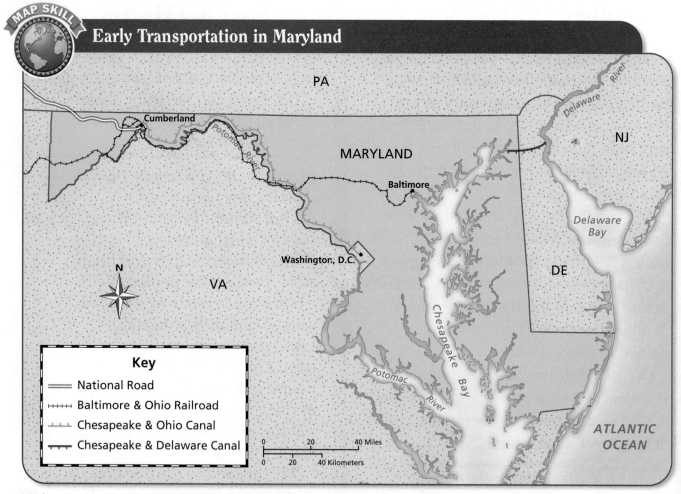

MAP SKILL

Early Transportation in Maryland

Key
- ══ National Road
- ┼┼┼ Baltimore & Ohio Railroad
- ┴┴┴ Chesapeake & Ohio Canal
- ┬┬┬ Chesapeake & Delaware Canal

▶ Roads, canals, and railroads made Maryland a transportation center for the nation in the early 1800s.

MAP SKILL Use Routes *Which of the four routes goes to and from Washington, D.C.?*

In addition to the National Road, Marylanders wanted to improve water travel. Years before, President George Washington had the idea of building canals on the Potomac River that would allow boats to go around rapids and waterfalls. Marylanders liked his idea because shipping by water was less expensive and more efficient than shipping by land.

In 1828 construction began on the Chesapeake and Ohio Canal. The canal system would link Washington, D.C., and the Ohio River valley.

The completed canal did not reach the Ohio River valley, though. Boats could travel only from Washington, D.C., to Cumberland. Even though the Chesapeake and Ohio Canal did not stretch as far west as Marylanders would have liked, it became an important commercial waterway to carry Maryland's farm and forest products to markets.

In 1829 another canal opened in the eastern part of Maryland. The Chesapeake and Delaware Canal linked cities on the northern part of Chesapeake Bay with the Delaware River. You can trace both canals on the map on page 68.

The canal boats were more than 90 feet long and could carry up to 120 tons of cargo. The canals were six feet deep and up to 60 feet wide. The locks were wide enough for only one boat to pass through at a time. A team of mules slowly pulled the boats along the canal. Goods such as coal and corn could now be shipped for less money.

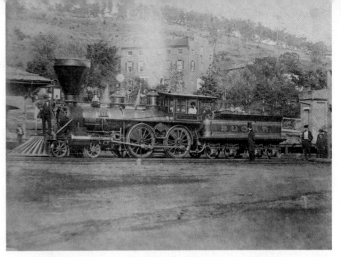

▶ The steam locomotive, called the iron horse, brought a faster and more powerful form of transportation to Maryland.

About the same time that the Chesapeake and Ohio Canal opened, the nation's first passenger train traveled from east to west on Maryland's Baltimore and Ohio Railroad. The steam locomotive, sometimes called the **iron horse,** could travel only 20 miles per hour. Compared to a wagon traveling along the National Road or a canal boat being pulled by mules, the train was much faster.

REVIEW What advantages did each new form of transportation give Marylanders? **Compare and Contrast**

▶ Way stations, or places to eat and rest, welcomed travelers along the National Road.

Writers in History

While Maryland was fighting for independence and discovering new ways to travel, some Marylanders were writing it all down so that future generations would understand what life was once like in "The Old Line State." Maryland authors have written many famous stories, poems, and essays that describe their unique ideas and experiences. Frederick Douglass wrote about his experiences as an enslaved person.

Edgar Allan Poe, who spent many years living in

▶ Frederick Douglass wrote important essays and true stories that educated people about the harms of slavery.

Baltimore, wrote stories and poems to entertain readers. His dark tales of suspense still send chills up the spines of his readers. Baltimore-born Upton Sinclair and Leon Uris were authors of best-selling books.

REVIEW Summarize the different kinds of writing that Maryland authors have used. ⟳ **Summarize**

Summarize the Lesson

○— **1812** The War of 1812 began.

○— **1813** The British attacked Havre de Grace.

└ **1814** Francis Scott Key wrote "Defense of Fort McHenry."

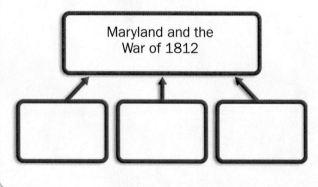

▶ Edgar Allan Poe wrote spine-tingling short stories of mystery and suspense.

LESSON 3 REVIEW

Check Facts and Main Ideas

1. **Main Idea and Details** On a separate sheet of paper, fill in the diagram to show the names of the three cities in or near Maryland where battles were fought during the War of 1812.

> Maryland and the War of 1812

2. What were the economic and political causes for the War of 1812?
3. Why was Baltimore blockaded during the War of 1812?
4. Who were two important writers in Maryland's history?
5. **Critical Thinking:** *Analyze* Describe three reasons that Maryland grew and prospered after the War of 1812.

Link to 〰 Geography

Make a Map Conduct research to find out more about the National Road in Maryland. Then draw a map of it and include four Maryland communities along the route.

Francis Scott Key

1779–1843

Francis Scott Key enjoyed hearing poetry and singing hymns when he was a boy. As an adult, he remembered how well these writers had described their feelings. When something inspired him, Key also wrote words to describe his feelings.

Francis Scott Key was a successful lawyer when the War of 1812 began. He loved his country very much, but he did not like the idea of another war.

When news reached him that an old friend had been captured by the British, Key boarded a British ship to meet with the British commanders. He persuaded them to release his friend. But Key saw the British preparing to attack Fort McHenry. The British decided that he knew too much to be released until the battle ended.

BIOFACT

Key's poem about the American flag was set to the tune of a popular British song.

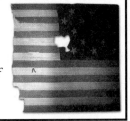

Throughout the long day and night, Key watched and listened to the battle at Fort McHenry. Bombs exploded, as rockets streaked through the smoke-filled air. Key knew that as long as the fighting continued, the battle was not lost. At dawn, the scene was quiet. As the sky cleared, Key saw the U.S. battle flag flying high.

Full of joy, Key grabbed a pen and a scrap of paper and started writing a poem. After his release, he continued writing and finished the poem in his Baltimore hotel room. At first, it was called "Defense of Fort McHenry." But in time, the poem became known as— "The Star-Spangled Banner."

Learn from Biographies

Why did Francis Scott Key write the words that became the national anthem?

Students can research the lives of significant people by clicking on *Meet the People* at **www.sfsocialstudies.com**.

1860   **1865**

1861	1862	1864	1865
The Civil War begins.	The Battle of Antietam is fought.	Maryland abolishes slavery.	The Civil War ends.

MARYLAND

Antietam Creek
• Frederick

A Divided Maryland

PREVIEW

Focus on the Main Idea
Maryland was divided over the issue of slavery during the Civil War.

PLACES
Frederick
Antietam Creek

PEOPLE
Harriet Tubman
Abraham Lincoln

VOCABULARY
emancipation

EVENTS
Baltimore Riot
Battle of Antietam

▶ Clara Barton collected medical supplies and treated the wounded during the Civil War. Her work was the beginning of the American Red Cross.

You Are There

"Are you scared?" you ask your sister as you watch her pack. "A little," she answers. "But Miss Barton and the soldiers need my help."

Tomorrow morning your sister is leaving to help Clara Barton nurse the soldiers on the Civil War battlefields. Miss Barton's work is very important. Some call her the "angel of the battlefield." She began her work by getting donated medical supplies. Before this, there were not enough supplies to treat wounded soldiers. Miss Barton goes right on to the battlefield and cares for the soldiers! Your sister and many other young women have signed on to help her. You will miss your sister, but you know that Miss Barton and the soldiers need her. And you are proud of her courage!

Summarize As you read, summarize how Marylanders participated in the Civil War.

Target Skill

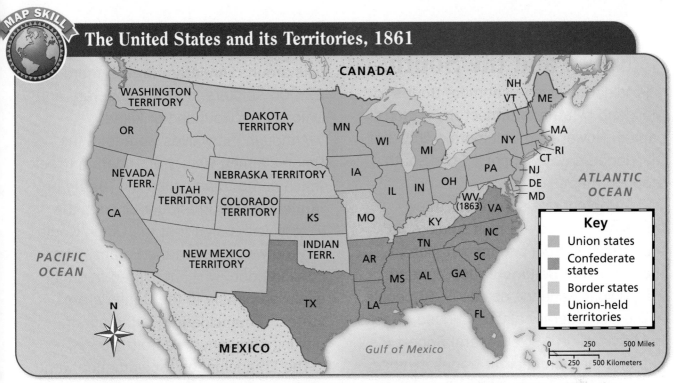

The United States and its Territories, 1861

Key
- Union states
- Confederate states
- Border states
- Union-held territories

▶ The Civil War divided the United States between the Union and the Confederate States of America.

Location *Why did Maryland's location cause it to be a border state during the Civil War?*

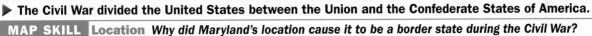

A Divided State

To many the Civil War was a fight about slavery. But it was also a battle to decide if states or the national government had more power. When the war began in 1861, the question of slavery divided Marylanders.

You have read in Chapter 1 that Maryland is "a state in the middle," between the Northern states and the Southern states. In many ways, Maryland was like a Northern state in the Union. Baltimore was a busy trade center and did not have plantations. Many people there and in the Appalachian Mountain region opposed slavery. Few people in the mountain region were slave holders. Some Marylanders, such as **Harriet Tubman,** even worked to help enslaved people escape to Northern states where they could be free.

However, many other Marylanders owned tobacco plantations and used enslaved people for labor. Their lives were more like those of plantation owners in the Southern Confederate states. They believed that enslaved workers were necessary for their way of life.

President **Abraham Lincoln** wanted Maryland to stay in the Union. If Maryland joined the Confederacy, Washington, D.C., would be cut off. Lincoln quickly sent Union soldiers to protect the capital.

REVIEW Give a brief summary of why Maryland was called a divided state during the Civil War. ⟳ Summarize

Fighting for the North and the South

President Lincoln sent more troops to Maryland by train to protect the nation's capital. However, in Baltimore a crowd of Marylanders who supported the South stopped them.

The Confederate supporters threw bricks and stones at Union soldiers as they marched from one train station to the next. The **Baltimore Riot** caused many injuries and the deaths of 16 people.

The Confederacy also continued attacks in Maryland. In 1862 General Robert E. Lee and the Confederate troops invaded the North. They crossed the Potomac River and camped near the town of **Frederick.** General George McClellan and his troops defended the Union position.

The armies also met in other battles in Maryland. In 1862 near the town of Sharpsburg, they fought one of the deadliest battles of the Civil War. On the hills around **Antietam Creek,** more than 23,000 soldiers, both Confederate and Union, were wounded or killed.

Although many lives were lost, the Union claimed victory at Antietam Creek which came to be called the **Battle of Antietam.** For President Lincoln, the victory was a sign that the Union would win the war. He read the Emancipation Proclamation, which declared free all enslaved people in the Confederate states. **Emancipation** is the act of making someone free from slavery.

The Emancipation Proclamation went into effect on January 1, 1863. Enslaved people in the border states were still not free, however. Despite the Union victory at Antietam, battles continued in Maryland. The state remained divided.

▶ **The Battle of Antietam was one of the bloodiest battles in U.S. history.**

Major Civil War Battles in Maryland

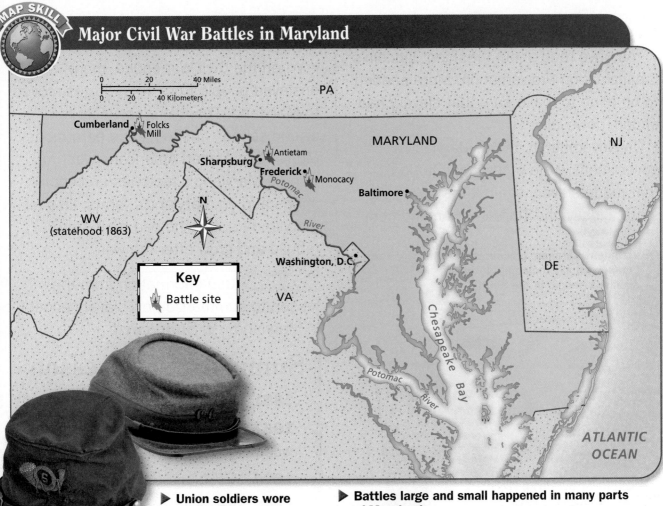

0 20 40 Miles

0 20 40 Kilometers

PA

Cumberland · Folcks Mill

Antietam

Sharpsburg

Frederick · Monocacy

MARYLAND

NJ

Baltimore ·

WV (statehood 1863)

N

Potomac River

Key
Battle site

Washington, D.C.

VA

DE

Chesapeake Bay

Potomac River

ATLANTIC OCEAN

▶ Union soldiers wore blue uniforms, and Confederate soldiers wore gray uniforms.

▶ Battles large and small happened in many parts of Maryland.

MAP SKILL Location *Which battle was fought closest to Baltimore?*

You have read about Maryland's Chesapeake and Ohio Canal and the Baltimore and Ohio Railroad. The Union and the Confederacy both wanted these important routes to move their troops and supplies west. Each side fought for control, but Union troops eventually won.

Marylanders continued to fight for their causes in the eastern part of the state, as well. Citizens who supported the Confederacy crossed Chesapeake Bay in small boats to smuggle supplies to Virginia, a Confederate state.

After four years of fighting, the Civil War ended in 1865. The war that had divided Maryland was finally over. Slavery was abolished, or done away with, and the states remained as one nation.

Tragically, John Wilkes Booth, a supporter of the Confederacy, could not accept defeat. He shot President Lincoln and escaped, but he was chased and later killed in Virginia.

REVIEW How were the goals of the supporters of the Confederacy and the supporters of the Union alike? How were they different? **Compare and Contrast**

75

Slavery Ends

You have read about President Lincoln's Emancipation Proclamation. More needed to be done to make sure that slavery had ended, however.

On November 1, 1864, Maryland's government wrote a new constitution that made slavery against the law in the state. Finally, the Thirteenth Amendment to the U.S. Constitution in 1865 made slavery illegal in all states.

When the Civil War ended, many enslaved people from other states moved to Maryland. They were now able to attend school, find jobs, and earn money. Many freed African Americans went to work in Maryland's factories and coal mines and on Maryland's farms. Like all Marylanders, they helped their state rebuild and grow after the war.

▶ **President Abraham Lincoln issued the Emancipation Proclamation that freed enslaved people in the South.**

REVIEW Use information from the lesson to summarize how slavery ended in Maryland. ◌ **Summarize**

Summarize the Lesson

- **1861** The Civil War began.
- **1862** The Battle of Antietam was fought.
- **1864** Maryland abolished slavery.
- **1865** The Civil War ended.

LESSON 4 ⟩ REVIEW

Check Facts and Main Ideas

1. ◌ Summarize On a separate sheet of paper, fill in the diagram with details to support the statement.

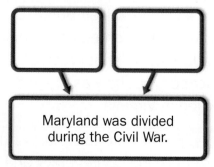

Maryland was divided during the Civil War.

2. Why did Maryland stay in the Union?
3. Why was the Battle of Antietam the most important Civil War battle fought in Maryland?
4. What happened in Maryland when the war ended?
5. **Critical Thinking: *Cause and Effect*** What effect did the Civil War have on different parts of Maryland?

Link to ⌘⌘ Writing

Write a Travel Article Write a story for a Maryland travel magazine describing the historic Civil War locations that are now tourist attractions in Maryland.

Harriet Tubman
about 1820–1913

By the time Harriet Tubman was five years old, she was working on a Maryland plantation as an enslaved person. If she did not do what she was told, her owners punished her. When Harriet was 15 years old, she tried to help another slave escape. When her owners found out, she was beaten. She knew that she had to escape too.

Tubman was about 30 years old when she left the plantation on her long journey. She traveled 90 miles alone, north to the Mason-Dixon Line. When she crossed into Pennsylvania, she was free.

Harriet Tubman, named Araminta at birth, later changed her name. Enslaved people were identified by tags such as this.

Later, she helped other enslaved people escape using the Underground Railroad. The Underground Railroad was a secret path for people who wanted to escape slavery. The slow, difficult journey took Tubman and others through woods and swamps. Many brave people hid them in their homes.

Tubman continued to help others. She went back to Maryland at least 19 times as a "conductor" to lead hundreds of other enslaved people to freedom. Plantation owners offered a $40,000 reward to anyone who could capture Tubman.

Harriet Tubman was famous for her courage. During the Civil War, she served as both a nurse and a spy for the Union troops. Tubman became a symbol for bravery and courage for many Americans.

Learning from Biographies

What are some examples of Harriet Tubman's bravery?

Students can research the lives of significant people by clicking on *Meet the People* at **www.sfsocialstudies.com.**

Use a Battle Map

What? You have read that Maryland's location made it a divided state during the Civil War. Both Union and Confederate troops used battle maps to understand the land on which they would be fighting. A battle map shows the location of battle sites, as well as important landforms, waterways, and nearby cities.

Why? During the Civil War, generals of both armies used maps to plan how long it would take to travel from one location to another. Maps also helped them learn about the landforms and waterways on which they would be fighting. They had to know the next location for supplies, the next place to camp, and the next location for a battle.

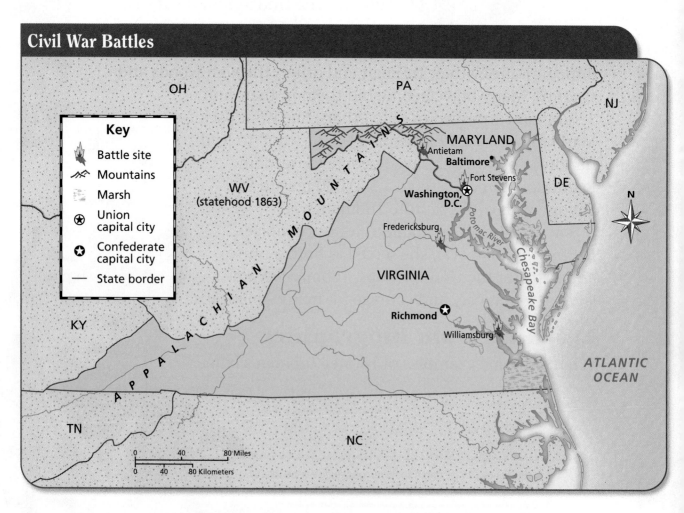

Civil War Battles

Key
- Battle site
- Mountains
- Marsh
- Union capital city
- Confederate capital city
- State border

OH
PA
NJ
MARYLAND
Antietam
Baltimore
WV (statehood 1863)
Fort Stevens
DE
Washington, D.C.
N
Fredericksburg
Potomac River
Chesapeake Bay
VIRGINIA
KY
Richmond
Williamsburg
ATLANTIC OCEAN
TN
NC
APPALACHIAN MOUNTAINS

0   40   80 Miles
0   40   80 Kilometers

They also had to know if they would need to cross a river, fight on marshy land, or climb over mountains. If the generals did not plan carefully, they could lose the battles. Using a battle map will help you understand why Civil War battles were fought in these locations.

How? To use a battle map, first determine what area is shown. Read the map's title. Then read the map key or legend. The map on page 78 shows Civil War capitals, the Potomac River, Chesapeake Bay, the Appalachian Mountains, marshes, and some of the war's major battlefields in Maryland and Virginia.

Find Washington, D.C., the Union's capital. In Virginia, find Richmond, the capital of the Confederacy. Now find the four Civil War battles on the map:

Antietam, Fort Stevens, Fredericksburg, and Williamsburg. Use your ruler and the map scale to find out how many miles it is from one site to another.

Look again at the four battle sites. Use the map key to find out what the land was like where the Union and Confederate soldiers fought. Also look for nearby rivers that they might have had to cross, or wet marshy land near the battle sites that might have made fighting more difficult. How might battle sites near the edge of mountains affect armies?

Think and Apply

1. How far is the Union capital, Washington, D.C., from Richmond, the capital of the Confederacy?

2. Which battle took place near mountains?

3. Which major battle was fought closest to the Confederate capital?

▶ **Richmond, Virginia, served as the capital of the Confederate States of America. The capitol in Richmond is shown in the picture at the left.**

For more information, go online to the *Atlas* at **www.sfsocialstudies.com.**

1850　　　　1900　　　　1950

1877
The Great Railroad
Strike takes place.

1917
The United
States enters
World War I.

1941
The United
States enters
World War II.

MARYLAND

Baltimore

PREVIEW

Focus on the Main Idea
After the Civil War, Baltimore continued to grow, becoming one the largest cities in the United States.

PLACE
Baltimore

PEOPLE
Franklin Delano Roosevelt

VOCABULARY
cannery
strike
depression

EVENTS
Oyster Wars
Great Railroad Strike
World War I
World War II

▶ New immigrants to Maryland often carried all their belongings in trunks like the one below.

Growth and Conflicts

You Are There

June 1890
Dear Grandma,
We are finally in America! Baltimore is a big city with tall buildings and a busy harbor. Our steamship has already sailed back to Europe.

I didn't feel very well when we arrived at Locust Point. Dad said the seasickness would go away once I was back on land, and it did.

We are living in a small apartment in a busy neighborhood of people from many countries. We don't have much time to play. We all have to work to earn money. Mom sews for a clothing factory. Dad works on the docks. I work in the cannery putting seafood into cans. It is not easy to be a stranger in a new land.

Summarize As you read, summarize the ways that Maryland and its cities grew and became strong.

Target Skill

Immigration and Growth

As you read in Chapter 1, Maryland's natural resources provide a variety of important products. After the Civil War ended, **Baltimore** used these resources to become one of the most successful cities in the United States.

Marylanders built ships, made clothing, grew crops, and mined coal. Ships from Baltimore's harbor moved these goods from Maryland to the rest of the world. The B&O Railroad transported Maryland's products across the United States.

Some food products were canned before being shipped. Oysters and other seafood were sent to a **cannery,** a factory where food is canned. The city of Crisfield, Maryland, became known as the Seafood Capital of the Country, because of its canneries. Like Baltimore, Crisfield benefited from its location on Chesapeake Bay.

Businesses boomed in the late 1800s. Immigrants arrived in Baltimore to fill the many jobs that were available. Many parents and even their children worked in the canneries.

Between 1870 and 1900, Maryland's population grew by more than 50 percent. Immigrants came to Maryland and other states on the East Coast from around the world. Most immigrants during this period came from Germany, Ireland, Russia, and Poland. The hard work of immigrants helped make Baltimore a thriving business center.

REVIEW Summarize the ways that immigrants helped Baltimore grow.

🄪 Summarize

▶ Maryland's canneries attracted immigrant workers who came to the state in large numbers in the late 1800s.

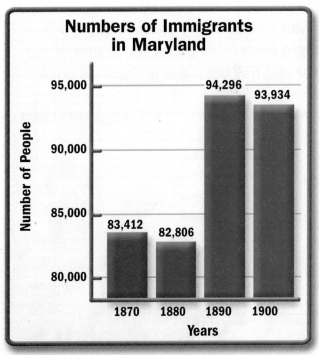

Numbers of Immigrants in Maryland

Number of People

Years	
1870	83,412
1880	82,806
1890	94,296
1900	93,934

▶ The late 1800s and early 1900s were years when many immigrants came to Maryland.

GRAPH SKILL *What year shown on the graph had the fewest immigrants?*

Labor Conflicts

With the increased population came more problems, especially with workers. In many industries workers wanted better working conditions and higher pay for long hours on the job.

Many of Baltimore's workers decided to **strike,** or stop work in protest, until they could earn more money and work fewer hours. Some workers marched in the streets with posters so that others would know about their unfair treatment.

People who fished, or watermen, hauled in huge numbers of fish, oysters, and crabs from Chesapeake Bay and the Potomac River. Sailing out in skipjack boats, watermen could bring in ten million bushels of oysters each year. Oysters became a source of great wealth, so watermen wanted to protect their oyster territories.

Watermen in Maryland and Virginia fought each other about which part of the river and bay belonged to them as private fishing areas. The Potomac, especially, was known to be one of the world's best breeding areas for oysters.

In the 1870s and 1880s, watermen from both states sailed out and raided each other's oyster beds. During these **Oyster Wars,** gunfire often broke out as the raiders met. Fighting continued for many years. The Potomac Fisheries Bill, signed in 1962, stated that the Potomac River would be governed by a committee of representatives from both Maryland and Virginia. The committee would govern the river's rich oyster beds.

Another conflict involved the B&O Railroad in Maryland. From Baltimore the railroad transported Maryland's goods as far as Chicago. Workers were also laying new tracks to other cities. Many Marylanders worked for the railroad.

But in time labor problems caused the first major strike in the United States. The **Great Railroad Strike** started in Baltimore in 1877.

▶ **Watermen from Maryland and Virginia often raided one another's oyster beds.**

▶ **Marylanders went on strike when they asked for better working conditions but did not get them.**

Many workers thought that their jobs on the railroad were too dangerous. They worked long hours in terrible conditions. When their already low wages were cut even more, the workers called for a strike.

Strikers and their supporters threw stones and burned one of the train's passenger cars. At one point, many people rioted in the streets. The governor of Maryland sent a message to the President of the United States asking that troops be sent to protect Baltimore. State and federal troops arrived and ended the riots. Before the fighting was over, though, ten people had died.

Even children had labor problems. You have read that many children worked in Baltimore canneries. Often these child workers did not go to school. Then, in the early 1900s, Marylanders passed laws that stopped children under the age of 12 from working in factories. Working conditions for all Marylanders slowly began to improve.

REVIEW What were the conditions that caused Marylanders to strike? **Cause and Effect**

World Conflicts

In 1917 Maryland, along with the rest of the United States, turned its attention to conflicts in other parts of the world. Several countries in Europe, including Germany, were competing with one another for land, trade, and military power. When Germany began to threaten the United States, the United States declared war and entered **World War I.**

Marylanders worked to help win the war against Germany. Baltimore was an important shipbuilding port. To support the war effort, many Marylanders built ships to take American troops across the Atlantic Ocean. Although the ships carried troops from all parts of the country, more than 60,000 soldiers in World War I were from Maryland.

Marylanders also used their own boats to help the war effort. Boats that usually collected oysters off the shore now had another important job. Oyster boats patrolled the ocean, watching for German submarines that might try to attack the United States.

Even the canneries in Maryland helped the war effort. Marylanders already shipped canned foods to other parts of the country. Now those canned foods were sent to troops across the Atlantic Ocean in Europe.

▶ **Marylanders joined the military and shipped off to Europe to fight in World War I.**

You have read about Fort McHenry's important role during the War of 1812. During World War I, Fort McHenry opened its doors to the wounded. It became a military hospital, treating more than 20,000 wounded American soldiers brought home from Europe.

By 1919 more than 40 new buildings had been carefully built around the original fort. Construction workers needed to be sure that any historical structures from the War of 1812 were not harmed.

The United States troops helped win World War I. After the war Marylanders and other Americans enjoyed good times for about ten years.

However, in 1929 the United States entered the Great Depression. A **depression** is a period of economic difficulty that results in lost jobs and slow business. Even many wealthy people lost the money that they had saved. **Franklin Delano Roosevelt** became President during these difficult times and used federal money to start job programs.

Although the programs helped, many Americans were still out of work. People came to Baltimore looking for jobs but found few opportunities. It was a hard time for Maryland and the nation.

People in parts of Europe and Japan were also experiencing hard times. Some of their leaders wanted to control other countries. These leaders said this would end the hard times. Certain countries agreed to protect each other in the event that their land was invaded by these leaders. When invasions started, a second world war began. In 1941 Japan attacked a U.S. naval base at Pearl Harbor, Hawaii. In response, the United States entered **World War II.**

Once again, Marylanders helped the nation in the battles overseas. More than 240,000 Marylanders served in the army or navy. Marylanders at home did their part too. Some built supply ships and airplanes. Others found a way to store drinking water, keeping it safe for long periods of time. Volunteers along the coast watched for enemy planes.

Maryland's men and women who were not serving in the military worked in factories to keep the economy growing. By the time World War II ended, the economy was strong again.

REVIEW Summarize how Marylanders helped their nation during two world wars.
⊙ Summarize

▶ Women at home joined in the war effort by working in shipyards and factories.

BOYS and GIRLS!
You can Help your Uncle Sam Win the War

W.S.S.

Save your Quarters
BUY WAR SAVINGS STAMPS

▶ To help pay for the war effort, Marylanders bought savings stamps.

Into the Future

During World War II, many people came to Baltimore and the Washington, D.C., area to work in factory and government jobs. When the war ended, many people stayed. Maryland's population grew very quickly. Its economy grew as well. People built thousands of new houses in and around Baltimore. With money from the government, returning soldiers attended school to learn new skills.

Today Maryland's economy benefits from high-tech industries, improved communication, and government service jobs. Marylanders work in space centers, medical research labs, and computer technology businesses. Super highways, planes, and high-tech communications link our state to the rest of the world.

Marylanders also joined together to rebuild the Baltimore harbor area, which had lost business and become polluted.

FACT FILE

Higher Learning in Maryland

Maryland's institutions of higher learning help train many of our state's young people for future jobs.

▶ Students at St. Mary's College have safety goggles to protect their eyes in a biology lab.

▶ A student uses the lobby of the art-sociology building for studying at the University of Maryland.

▶ Homewood House is one of the beautiful buildings on the campus of Johns Hopkins University.

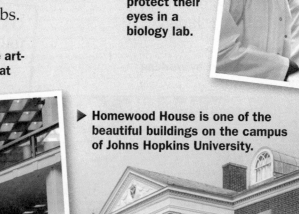

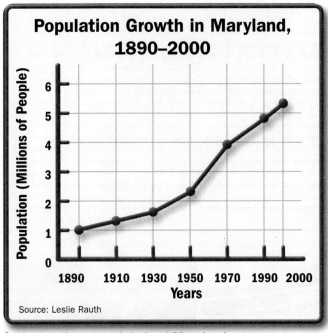

Population Growth in Maryland, 1890–2000

Source: Leslie Rauth

▶ Population growth helped Maryland prosper.

GRAPH SKILL *Which period had the largest population increase?*

Now it is an exciting center for tourism and the home of many big corporations.

Today the state is also working to improve other parts of its environment.

The Chesapeake Bay clean-up efforts are helping people learn how to protect the bay from further pollution.

The state is also helping some people improve their living conditions and make their neighborhoods safer. Marylanders know that by working together they can solve these problems, as they have solved other problems in the past.

REVIEW What changes have taken place in Maryland since WWII? ⟳ Summarize

Summarize the Lesson

1877 The Great Railroad Strike took place.

1917 The United States entered World War I.

1941 The United States entered World War II.

LESSON 5 ❯ REVIEW

Check Facts and Main Ideas

1. ⟳ Summarize On a separate sheet of paper, fill in a diagram like the one below to summarize how immigrants helped Maryland grow in the late 1800s.

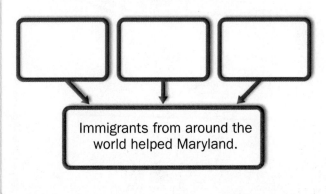

2. What challenges did workers face in the late 1800s?

3. What caused the Great Railroad Strike of 1877?

4. How did Maryland industries and the state's military personnel help the nation win two world wars?

5. **Critical Thinking:** *Cause and Effect* Why did Maryland's growth speed up after World War II, and what problem did that growth cause?

Research Inventions Many new inventions were created during World War II. Research to find a wartime invention, and share a description and pictures of the invention with the class.

Then and Now

Transportation and Communication

Marylanders built the National Road and laid tracks for the nation's first passenger railroad. Today superhighways make travel easy, and satellite communication has replaced the telegraph.

▶ Modern Presidents travel by jet plane.

▶ Marylanders helped build the nation's first U.S. highway.

▶ George Washington, our first President, often traveled by horseback.

▶ Today's superhighways carry millions of vehicles.

▶ Satellites speed up communications.

▶ Telephones continued to improve as technology improved.

▶ At one time, telegraphs were modern communication systems.

▶ The earliest telephones were once considered high-tech.

▶ Today cellular telephones transmit messages without using wires.

Chapter Summary

Summarize

Target Skill

On a separate sheet of paper, fill in the diagram to summarize ways that Marylanders supported their state and nation throughout history.

```
┌──────┐  ┌──────┐  ┌──────┐
│      │  │      │  │      │
└───┬──┘  └───┬──┘  └───┬──┘
    │         │         │
    ▼         ▼         ▼
   ┌────────────────────────┐
   │  Marylanders supported │
   │  their state and nation.│
   └────────────────────────┘
```

Main Ideas and Skills

1. **Main Idea** From where did the first people to settle in the lands of what is now Maryland come?

2. **Main Idea** What was it like to live in colonial Maryland for people who were free and for people who were enslaved?

3. **Main Idea** How did Marylanders help win the Revolutionary War and the War of 1812?

4. **Main Idea** What caused Maryland to be divided during the Civil War?

5. **Critical Thinking:** *Cause and Effect* How did Maryland's unique location play a role in historical events in the 1860s?

Apply Skills

6. **Use a Battle Map** What important information on a battle map helped generals plan their actions?

Vocabulary and Places

Match each word with a correct definition or description.

1. **tolerance** (p. 52)
2. **blockade** (p. 65)
3. **impressment** (p. 65)
4. **strike** (p. 82)
5. **depression** (p. 85)

a. sailor kidnapping and forced military service

b. to stop work in protest

c. the stopping of ships from entering a port

d. a period of economic difficulty

e. respect for others

Write a sentence about each of the following places.

6. St. Mary's City (p. 54)
7. Chester Town (p. 59)
8. Annapolis (p. 62)
9. Fort McHenry (p. 66)
10. Antietam Creek (p. 74)

Write About History

1. **Write a diary entry** as if you were a young indentured servant working in colonial Maryland.

2. **Write a news report** about the victory at Fort McHenry during the War of 1812.

3. **Write a list of instructions** to help guide an enslaved person escaping on the Underground Railroad.

Living in Maryland

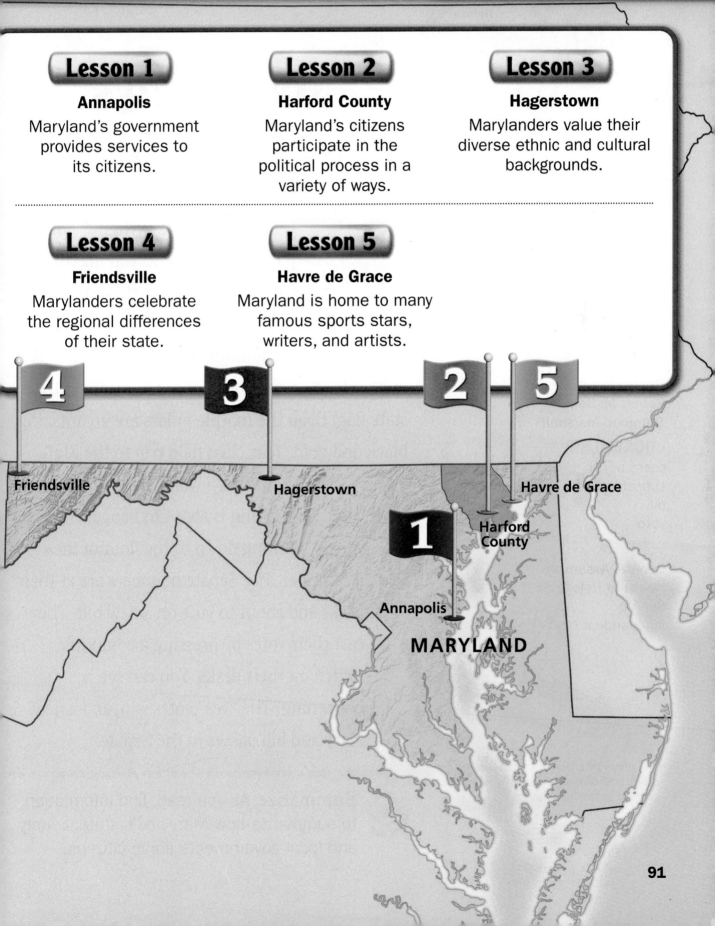

CHAPTER 3

Lesson 1

Annapolis

Maryland's government provides services to its citizens.

Lesson 2

Harford County

Maryland's citizens participate in the political process in a variety of ways.

Lesson 3

Hagerstown

Marylanders value their diverse ethnic and cultural backgrounds.

Lesson 4

Friendsville

Marylanders celebrate the regional differences of their state.

Lesson 5

Havre de Grace

Maryland is home to many famous sports stars, writers, and artists.

4

3

2

5

Friendsville

Hagerstown

Havre de Grace

1

Harford County

Annapolis

MARYLAND

MARYLAND

Frederick County

Baltimore •
Annapolis •

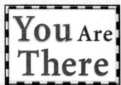

PREVIEW

Focus on the Main Idea
Maryland's state, county, and local governments provide services to citizens.

PLACES
Baltimore
Annapolis
Frederick County

PEOPLE
Robert M. Bell
Thurgood Marshall

VOCABULARY
secretary
subcabinet
bill
veto

TERMS
General Assembly
House of Delegates
Senate
independent city

▶ A gavel traditionally symbolizes the authority of those who keep order in the legislature.

Maryland's Government

You Are There

"Look up at the skylight," your teacher whispers. You lift your eyes and see light streaming through the multicolored glass. Your tour guide tells your class that all the colors you'll see today in Maryland's Senate Chamber are colors in the state flag. Even the marble pillars are an amazing black and gold. This class field trip to the State House in Annapolis was a wonderful idea.

"Watch! Something is about to happen," your teacher says pointing down to the floor of the Senate chamber. The Senate members are at their desks and about to vote on a new bill. They cast their votes by pressing a computer switch on their desks. You can see it happening! The "yes" votes win, and a new Maryland bill passes in the Senate!

Summarize As you read, find information to summarize how Maryland's state, county, and local governments serve citizens.

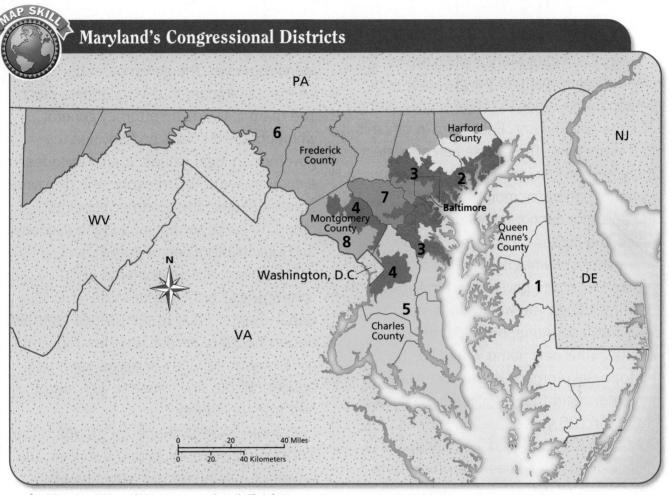

▶ Maryland has eight congressional districts.

MAP SKILL Locate *In which congressional district is Frederick County located?*

State, County, and City Governments

Maryland has state, county, and local governments. The people elect some government officials, but many others are not elected. Instead, governments hire them to help Maryland's people. Highway patrol officers, deputy sheriffs, and city firefighters are all government employees.

Each type of government follows a plan. Maryland's state government, for example, is a lot like the U.S. government.

Maryland elects representatives and senators to the U.S. Congress to help make U.S. laws. In Maryland's state government the governor, like the U.S. President, heads the executive branch. The state's **General Assembly** forms the legislative branch. Like the U.S. Congress, the Assembly has two parts. Together, Maryland's **House of Delegates** and **Senate** make state laws. Maryland's judicial branch interprets the laws, just as the U.S. court system does.

Maryland also has county and local governments. One city in Maryland, **Baltimore,** is an **independent city** that operates its own city government.

REVIEW How is Maryland's state government like that of the U.S. government? **Compare and Contrast**

The Executive Branch

Every four years Maryland's citizens elect officials, such as the governor and lieutenant governor, to the executive branch of state government. Each term in office is four years long. The people can also elect the governor for a second term, but no governor can serve more than two terms. If the governor cannot complete the term of office, the lieutenant governor takes over.

Think about what it would be like to be a member of the governor's family! One of the first things you would do is pack for your move to **Annapolis,** Maryland's capital. Your new home would be the historic Government House. Maryland's governors and their families have lived there for 125 years!

Maryland's State House in Annapolis is also historic—the oldest operating state capitol in the United States. Maryland's new governor would have an office in that historic building—and all the responsibilities that go with that important job. The governor sees that the day-to-day business of state government runs smoothly and that state laws are put into action. The governor cannot do all the jobs alone, however. The governor leads an executive team that Marylanders elect. The team includes an attorney general who upholds the laws and advises the governor on legal issues. It also includes a comptroller of the treasury, who oversees state finances. The governor appoints others to do important jobs in the executive and judicial branches of government.

The governor also appoints **secretaries,** or heads of state departments. Each of the state's eighteen departments is responsible for important government services in areas such as education, the environment, agriculture, and transportation.

To make sure that special groups within the state receive important services, the governor may also form **subcabinets,** or specialized departments. The Subcabinet for Children, Youth, and Families, for example, makes sure that Maryland's children are healthy and safe and have equal educational opportunities.

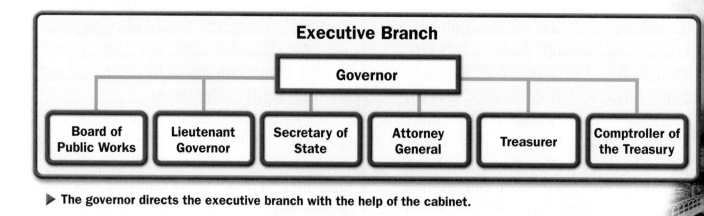

Executive Branch

Governor

| Board of Public Works | Lieutenant Governor | Secretary of State | Attorney General | Treasurer | Comptroller of the Treasury |

▶ The governor directs the executive branch with the help of the cabinet.

▶ Executive branch departments and agencies are responsible for the special needs of Maryland's citizens.

The governor, as the head of the executive branch, works with the state's legislative General Assembly. For example, part of the governor's job is to develop a state budget that shows how Maryland's money will be spent. This budget goes to the Assembly for approval. Assembly members review the budget, add their changes, and decide whether to approve it.

The General Assembly can also send a **bill,** or a proposed new law, to the governor. If the governor signs the bill, it becomes a law. However, the governor can also **veto,** or reject, a bill. A vetoed bill goes back to the General Assembly. The General Assembly can then vote to make the bill a law without the governor's signature.

REVIEW What are some of the important responsibilities of the executive branch? **Main Idea and Details**

▶ The Subcabinet for Children, Youth, and Families works to ensure that Maryland's children receive services from the state.

▶ People in Maryland expect basic services from their state government, including well-maintained highways.

The Legislative Branch

You have read that Maryland's legislative branch is called the General Assembly. Each year the General Assembly meets in the State House for 90 days, from January to April, to conduct state business and pass new laws.

The General Assembly has many additional responsibilities. The Assembly sets up departments for state services, and it may propose taxes to pay for services such as rebuilding highways. In some cases the Assembly proposes changes to the state constitution for Maryland's citizens to vote on in the next election.

The House of Delegates has 141 members, three delegates from each of the state's 47 election districts. Delegates must be at least 21 years old, have lived in the state for at least one year, and lived in the district for six months. They are elected for four-year terms. Delegates elect a House Speaker to oversee the House of Delegates sessions.

One senator is elected from each district to serve a four-year term. Senators must have lived in the state at least one year and in the district for six months and be at least 25 years old. Senators elect a Senate president annually to oversee their meetings.

▶ For 90 days each year, Maryland's State House welcomes senators and delegates from all parts of Maryland to the General Assembly.

Legislative Branch

General Assembly

House of Delegates

Senate

▶ Maryland's legislative branch proposes, debates, and may pass new state laws.

If you were living in the Government House, you might notice how busy Annapolis becomes during the General Assembly's 90-day session. Senators, delegates, and legislative staff develop, propose, and debate new bills. For a bill to be successful in the General Assembly, it must pass a vote in both the House and the Senate.

Bills might introduce new laws for taxes, education, or public safety, such as requiring people to wear helmets when riding motorcycles. Citizens may learn about these bills from the radio, newspapers, television, or the Department of Legislative Services. This department prints short descriptions of the bills for people to read. Some voters attend General Assembly meetings to support or oppose a bill.

In the House and Senate chambers, members explain why they think a bill should be passed or defeated. Sometimes a bill is held until a later time if it does not have enough votes to pass at that session. This extra time lets supporters of the bill try to win more votes.

REVIEW In what ways are the House of Delegates and Senate alike and different? **Compare and Contrast**

The Judicial Branch

Maryland's judicial branch of government has four different types of courts to serve Marylanders. The judicial branch makes sure that the laws passed by the General Assembly and signed by the governor are enforced fairly and do not violate the state constitution. Courts may hear civil cases, or disputes between people, and criminal cases, or cases about crimes.

Civil cases may involve lawsuits. For example, if someone has an automobile accident, that person may ask the other person to pay for damages to the car. The court must then decide whose fault the accident was and who must pay for repairs.

▶ Courts may not allow photographers to take pictures during a trial. Magazines and newspapers sometimes use sketches like this one when they report on a court case.

Courts also decide criminal cases. The higher courts hear cases of serious crimes, and the lower level court, or District Courts hear cases of less serious crimes. A person protesting a speeding ticket, for example, goes to a District Court.

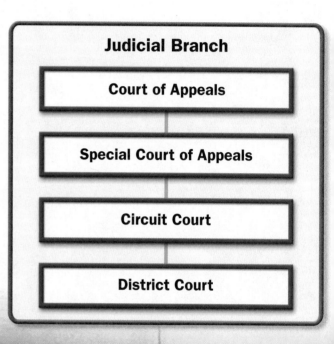

Judicial Branch

- Court of Appeals
- Special Court of Appeals
- Circuit Court
- District Court

In some of the state's courts, juries of citizens help judges decide what is fair. The high-level courts are called circuit courts. There is a Circuit Court for each county and for Baltimore City. The Circuit Court not only hears the more serious criminal and civil cases but also hears appeals, or requests to hear a case again, from decisions in the District Court.

Sometimes a Marylander is not happy with the decision of a district or circuit court. The person may think the case was presented unfairly or that some of the facts were overlooked. The person can then ask a higher court to make sure the decision was correct and fair.

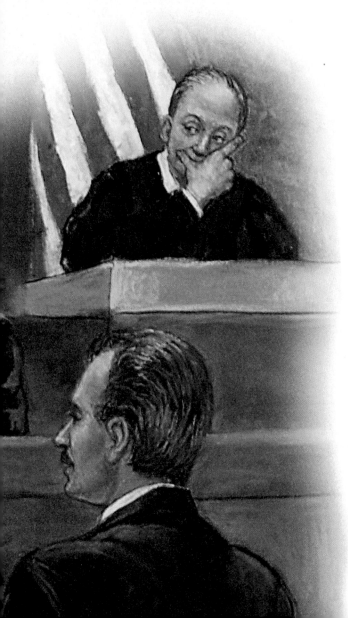

Maryland's higher courts hear most of the state cases that require another review.

Maryland's Court of Special Appeals hears most of the state cases that require another review. There are 13 judges of this court who serve for 10-year terms. An appealed case is usually presented to a group of three judges, but an important case will be heard by all 13 of the judges.

As Maryland's highest court, the Court of Appeals can pick the appeal cases they want to hear. These cases are important because they affect the meaning of the state constitution. If the Court of Appeals decides not to hear a case, the lower court's decision becomes final. There are seven judges of the Court of Appeals who serve for ten-year terms. The state constitution of 1776 says that judges on this court must be people "of integrity and sound judgment . . . whose judgment shall be final. . . ."

The chief judge of the Court of Appeals is the head of the Maryland judicial system. Chief Judge **Robert M. Bell,** the first African American to hold this important position in Maryland, was inspired by another Marylander, **Thurgood Marshall,** who served on the U.S. Supreme Court. You will read more about Thurgood Marshall in the biography on page 103.

The governor appoints the judges on both appeals courts with the agreement of the Senate. Then voters approve the choices during the next general election.

REVIEW How are Maryland's district courts and the Court of Appeals similar, and how are they different?
Compare and Contrast

County Government

For most Marylanders, local government means county government. They may know some of their county officials personally.

Maryland has 23 counties. Each county has a county seat, or city where county officials conduct local business and provide services. Counties have varied forms of government, but a council or county commissioners generally run counties. The city of Baltimore is neither in a county nor an official county by itself. However, Baltimore operates like a county.

Frederick County is a good example of how counties provide local government. Five commissioners elected by voters for four-year terms govern the county. The commissioners meet in the city of Frederick to carry out state laws, manage the local budget, and provide county services.

Frederick County wants its people to have important services available to them. The county commissioners manage community resources to provide libraries, parks, hospitals, water and sewage systems, and police and fire protection.

One of Frederick County's elected officials is the county sheriff, whose job is to help prevent crime and to protect people's lives and property. The sheriff and deputies help people in Frederick County stay safe.

At each Frederick County commission meeting, time is set aside for people to speak to the commissioners about their concerns. Citizens can participate in county government in many ways. They can attend work sessions, hearings, and planning committee meetings.

▶ County governments provide services, such as libraries, to Maryland's people.

▶ The Montgomery County Department of Park and Planning is responsible for Brookside Gardens.

100

Maryland's Counties and the City of Baltimore

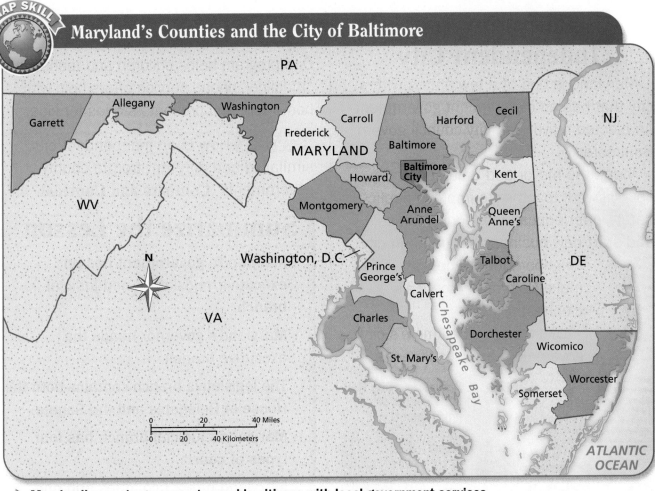

▶ Maryland's county goverments provide citizens with local government services.

MAP SKILL Understand Maryland's Counties *Which of Maryland's counties border Washington, D.C.?*

The county also has a Web site and a telephone access line. People can get information about county services and events there.

County governments rely on local citizens' participation. These governments receive their money from local taxpayers. When people have opinions about the actions of their county government, they want to have officials who listen to them. People also turn to their county governments for help when they have problems with things such as water quality, health, home building, and even animal control.

Counties also need people to voice their opinions about the plans and goals counties set for the area. Frederick County, like many other Maryland counties, has developed a countywide plan so that people can work together to make their county a better place to live.

Many other Maryland counties have similar ways of hearing citizens' views. In many ways, local county governments are the governments closest to the people they serve.

REVIEW How do citizens participate in county governments? ⭕ Summarize

Baltimore, the Independent City

Maryland is one of a few states with a city that has an independent government. An elected mayor and city council govern Baltimore.

Today, the mayor and Baltimore's city council work together to improve public safety, offer educational opportunities, and start new business programs in city neighborhoods. One goal is to make Baltimore America's cleanest city.

Like a county, Baltimore's city government provides libraries,

▶ Baltimore's City Hall is its center of government.

housing services, parks, emergency programs, and programs for senior citizens. One program helps children and teens. The "Kidsline" phone service offers help with homework and presents stories for kids.

REVIEW How is an independent city similar to and different from a county government? **Compare and Contrast**

Summarize the Lesson

- **Maryland's government has an executive, legislative, and judicial branch.**
- **Maryland's governor heads the executive branch.**
- **The legislative branch contains both the House of Delegates and the Senate.**
- **Maryland's judicial branch has four types of courts.**
- **Maryland has 23 counties and one independent city.**

LESSON 1 REVIEW

Check Facts and Main Ideas

1. **Summarize** On a separate sheet of paper, copy the graphic organizer and fill in five services that Maryland's local governments provide to citizens.

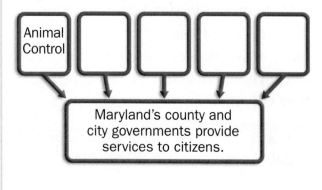

```
Animal
Control  →  [  ]  [  ]  [  ]  [  ]
              ↓    ↓    ↓    ↓
        Maryland's county and
        city governments provide
          services to citizens.
```

2. What are the three branches of Maryland's state government?
3. What is the General Assembly's main responsibility?
4. What are the roles of the executive, legislative, and judicial branches of state government?
5. **Critical Thinking: *Draw Conclusions*** How does the structure of Maryland's state government make sure that no one branch becomes too powerful?

Link to 👓 Writing

Write a Letter Write a letter to your senator to suggest a new law that increases safety for children.

102

Thurgood Marshall
1908–1993

Born in Baltimore, Thurgood Marshall was the great–grandson of an enslaved person. During the early 1900s, he attended a segregated Baltimore school. Segregated means "separated by race." Black children were sent to different, and often worse, schools than white children. Whenever his teacher sent him out of class for misbehaving, the principal made him read a section of the U.S. Constitution. In time, Thurgood would become an expert on constitutional law. His father took him to the local courthouse to watch trials. As a young man, he decided that becoming a lawyer would be a good way to help people receive fair and equal treatment.

After graduating from law school, Marshall began to question the laws that were unfair to African Americans. As a skilled lawyer, he helped win Supreme Court cases that gained rights for African Americans. His most famous victory was the 1954 case of *Brown* v. *Board of Education of Topeka, Kansas.* He represented parents who were suing the Topeka, Kansas, school board because their children were not allowed to go to the same schools as white children. He won his case, and segregation in public schools was no longer permitted. In 1967 President Lyndon Johnson named Thurgood Marshall the first African American Supreme Court Justice.

Learn from Biographies

What experiences that Thurgood Marshall had while growing up made him want to work for civil rights as an adult?

Students can research the lives of significant people by clicking on *Meet the People* at **www.sfsocialstudies.com**.

Understand a Flowchart

What? A flowchart is a picture of how something happens. It describes the steps in a process from beginning to end. A flowchart may show how an idea grows or develops into something finished or complete.

How a Bill Becomes a Law

1. Members of the House of Delegates or Senate write a bill.

2. The bill is passed to the other house for approval.

3. If the other house does not approve the bill, the bill ends.

STOP

4. The House of Delegates and the Senate approve the bill.

6. If the governor vetoes the bill, the bill returns to the legislature.

5. If the governor signs the bill, it becomes a law.

BILL

BILL

VETO

7. If a three-fifths majority in each of the House and the Senate vote for the bill again, it becomes a law without the governor's approval.

LAW

Why? Flowcharts give a clear, simple picture of how something moves in a process from beginning to end. Like other charts, a flowchart lets you see a lot of information at a glance. For example, a flowchart may show you the steps to follow to build a model airplane. It can be much easier to find the step you want on the flowchart than it is to read a paragraph or page to find the right step. Teachers often develop flowcharts to show students how to develop a science project or social studies report.

How? Always read the title of the flowchart. The title information tells you what process the flowchart is describing.

Look at the flowchart on page 104. Each square in the flowchart shows a step in the process of how a bill becomes a law in Maryland. Here are some questions that you could answer at a glance by using the flowchart. How many steps are in the process? How do the words and pictures help you understand each step? How does the flowchart show points where two different things might happen? What happens if the governor vetoes the bill?

▶ **Visitors may watch the actions of state legislators from the balconies of the capitol.**

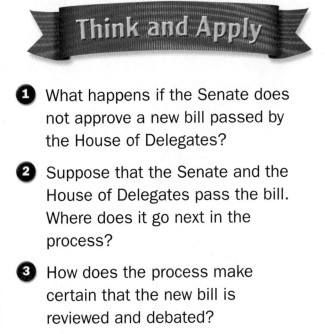

Think and Apply

1 What happens if the Senate does not approve a new bill passed by the House of Delegates?

2 Suppose that the Senate and the House of Delegates pass the bill. Where does it go next in the process?

3 How does the process make certain that the new bill is reviewed and debated?

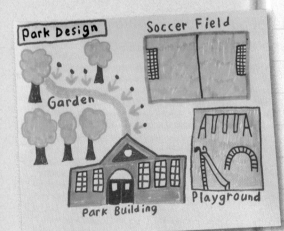

MARYLAND

Harford County

Chesapeake Bay

PREVIEW

Focus on the Main Idea
Marylanders participate in the political process in a variety of ways.

PLACE
Harford County

VOCABULARY
petition
ballot

TERMS
absentee ballot
primary election
general election
Project Citizen
Smart Growth Campaign

Park Design
Soccer Field
Garden
Park Building
Playground

▶ Some students work on service projects to design parks and gardens for their communities.

Citizenship in Maryland

You Are There
You race to catch up with your best friend after school. "Which park project group are you in? I'm on the Web site team! I get to use the new digital camera to take pictures of each step of the project." Everyone in your fourth-grade class thinks fixing up the community park is a good idea for the service project. Each week college students come to your school and help your class design a plan to clean up the park. You'll grow gardens, plant new bushes, build a playground, and hang birdhouses in the trees. And on the old park building, everyone is going to help paint a mural. At the meeting today, someone offered to tie a big red ribbon around the new swing set on opening day. What a great photo opportunity!

Summarize As you read, find information to summarize the ways that Marylanders participate in politics.

Citizen Participation

Marylanders of all ages help make Maryland a pleasant place to live. They care about their state and participate in a variety of ways.

Many Maryland citizens make phone calls to their lawmakers and attend Assembly meetings. Some citizens go door to door asking their neighbors to sign a **petition.** A petition is a written request to someone in authority for some right or privilege, often signed by many people, such as adding a traffic light to a busy intersection. These citizens then present the signed petitions to their government.

Marylanders know that they can make positive changes. When the Department of Recreation and Parks asked for volunteers for its Green Thunder Project, more than 400 citizens came to clean up litter and plant flowers in city parks. Volunteers picked up more than 100 tons of trash, and planted hundreds of flowers.

▶ This display is asking the government officials of Crisfield to help link the Eastern Shore to southern Maryland with a fast ferry.

Students like you can help in local service projects too. In Baltimore, students collected food items for people who do not have enough money for food. Students in Harford County planted grasses on the Chesapeake Bay shore and turned an abandoned lot into a community park. Marylanders of all ages participate as citizens.

REVIEW What are some of the ways Marylanders can practice citizenship in their neighborhoods? ⟳ Summarize

▶ People of all ages can help make their neighborhoods better places to live.

The Right to Vote

Maryland citizens vote to elect state, county, and city officials. They also vote to elect senators and legislators to represent them in the U.S. Congress. Every four years, Marylanders and citizens of other states vote to elect the President of the United States. Voting is both a right and a responsibility for Marylanders.

To be able to vote, a citizen must be at least 18 years old. Registering to vote is an important part of becoming an adult.

Election workers make certain that elections are fair by allowing people to vote only one time in each election. A voter may receive a **ballot,** or a way of casting a secret vote. Many Marylanders make their election choices in voting booths. In some cities Marylanders use computer screens instead of paper ballots to cast their votes.

Before an election Maryland's registered voters receive information about the people for whom they can vote, and where to go to vote. If a person cannot vote at his or her polling place because of illness, disability, or an out-of-town trip, he or she can request an **absentee ballot** to fill out and submit to be counted.

Marylanders vote in several different kinds of state elections. In a **primary election,** voters choose candidates for an upcoming general election. Every four years, voters elect their governor, senators, and legislators in a statewide **general election.** Baltimore holds its city elections the following year.

People in Maryland believe that government participation is not just for adults. It is also important for students to be active in their state and local governments.

▶ **These Marylanders are making their election choices.**

Elections in Maryland		
Election	**State Primary Election**	**State General Election**
Purpose	To choose state candidates for the General Election	To elect state leaders, including executives and legislators
Frequency	Once every four years in an even-numbered year	Once every four years in an even-numbered year
Month	September	November

▶ Citizens can work together to protect areas of Maryland, such as the coastal area.

Project Citizen is a hands-on education program that involves Maryland's middle school students. Students watch their government at work, and they make their opinions known to state leaders. Some students get their parents and other people in the community to sign on and help with their Project Citizen activities.

In Project Citizen, students select a problem in their community. They research what is causing the problem and interview people in the community. Then students figure out how the problem can be solved. Finally, they develop an action plan and present their plan in local and state competitions.

Students at George Fox Middle School in Pasadena, Maryland, know that working in Project Citizen can make a difference. Their hard work won awards at the Project Citizen National Showcase.

In 2001 those same students got the attention of Maryland's legislators with their public policy project, "Possible Dredge Spoil off the Coast of Pasadena." Their excellent report changed some legislators' minds. The legislators listened to the students and voted against using the coastal area as a dumping site.

REVIEW How can voting and citizen participation influence state leaders?
🔄 **Summarize**

FACT FILE

Contacting State Leaders

What if Marylanders have a question for one of their elected leaders? Maybe they want to know why the governor did not sign an important bill. Or they might want their legislator to know their opinion about a state bill coming up for a vote in the House of Delegates. In Maryland there are many ways to contact state leaders and make your voice heard.

▶ Writing letters to get information from state leaders is part of the Project Citizen process.

▶ Sending an e-mail is another way to contact your state leaders.

▶ Marylanders can call their state leaders on the telephone or send them fax messages.

Current Date

Your Senator, District #
Lowe House Office Building
Room 321
84 College Avenue
Annapolis, MD 21404-1991

Dear Senator:

The Smart Growth Campaign

As in many states, Maryland's population has grown in recent years. More people are now living in Maryland, especially in cities. The population has risen from 4 million to 5 million people in the last 30 years.

Population growth also means more houses and cars. For many Marylanders, it means long drives to work on crowded freeways. For Chesapeake Bay, growth threatens the water supply and the plants, animals, and people that depend on it.

Marylanders do not want growth to mean pollution and long hours on the freeway. Population growth can bring good things to the state, however, when growth is carefully planned by programs such as the **Smart Growth Campaign.**

The Smart Growth Campaign is an important way Marylanders can participate in state government. They can vote for preserving open spaces and fixing up urban areas so that people will want to live in the city near their jobs. Smart Growth also encourages Marylanders to clean up parks and waterways.

FACT FILE

Smart Growth Campaign

Maryland's Smart Growth Campaign gives cities and towns resources to make their communities better places to live. It preserves farmland and other natural resources. The goal of Smart Growth is to end sprawling housing developments that cause traffic problems and pollution.

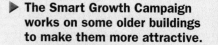

▶ The Smart Growth Campaign works on some older buildings to make them more attractive.

▶ Building new homes outside cities may mean the loss of wetlands that are important to wildlife.

▶ An important part of the Smart Growth Campaign is fixing up older neighborhoods in cities so that people will want to live there again.

► All over the state, in big cities and small towns, Marylanders make improvements as part of the Smart Growth Campaign.

In each area of Maryland, the Smart Growth Campaign asks citizens to develop local plans to control and wisely plan growth. People talk about what they want for their communities. They identify problems and make action plans to fix them.

Marylanders share their plans with their state leaders. Local citizen participation helps the state of Maryland develop a master plan to manage growth in positive ways.

REVIEW How do Marylanders participate in the Smart Growth Campaign? ⮌ Summarize

Summarize the Lesson

- **In Maryland, citizens of all ages participate to make Maryland a pleasant place to live.**
- **Marylanders vote in federal, state, county, and local elections.**
- **Marylanders develop Smart Growth plans for their communities.**

LESSON 2 REVIEW

Check Facts and Main Ideas

1. ⮌ Summarize On a separate sheet of paper, use the graphic organizer to summarize the ways that people can participate in the political process.

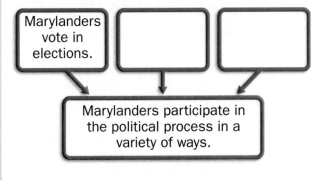

Marylanders vote in elections.

Marylanders participate in the political process in a variety of ways.

2. How can Marylanders get information that helps them participate in government?

3. What is the purpose of a primary election?

4. Why is it important that Maryland citizens participate in the Smart Growth Campaign?

5. **Critical Thinking: *Cause and Effect*** What are the effects of unplanned population growth in Maryland?

Link to ⚬⚬ Writing

Write a Report Using books, newspaper articles, and the Internet, research problems related to growth in your area. Write a report that describes how people work together for smarter growth.

Seeking the Right to Vote

On a January morning in 1648, Margaret Brent appeared before the Maryland General Assembly. She identified herself as both a landowner and a lawyer. She asked the Assembly to give her the right to vote.

The members of the Assembly were shocked. In the 1600s only men were allowed to vote. The Assembly was even more surprised when Brent asked not for just one vote, but two—one vote because she was a landowner and another vote because she was a lawyer for Lord Baltimore. As a tax-paying property owner, Margaret Brent believed that without the right to vote, she was being taxed without any way to make her views known to the government. She decided to fight for the right to vote.

In colonial times, Margaret Brent was considered an unusual woman. She never married, and she owned property. Educated in England, she came to North America as the head of her own household. On his deathbed Maryland's governor, Leonard Calvert, gave Margaret Brent, his sister-in-law, the power to "take all and pay all" after his death. Because she was taking care of Leonard Calvert's estate, she had asked the Provincial Court to also name her as attorney for Leonard's brother, Cecil Calvert, the second Lord Baltimore. Lord Baltimore was still in England, but the Maryland colony belonged to him. The court granted Brent's request.

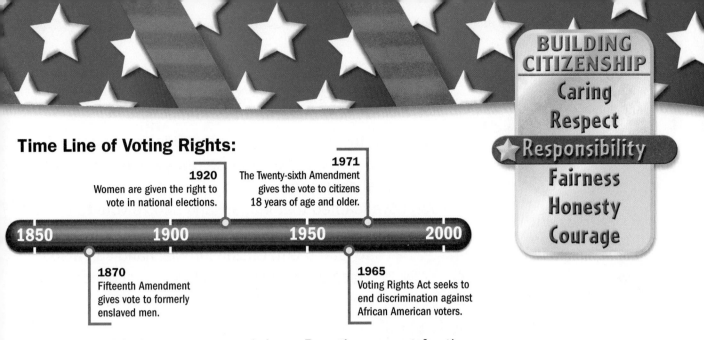

Time Line of Voting Rights:

1920
Women are given the right to vote in national elections.

1971
The Twenty-sixth Amendment gives the vote to citizens 18 years of age and older.

1850   1900   1950   2000

1870
Fifteenth Amendment gives vote to formerly enslaved men.

1965
Voting Rights Act seeks to end discrimination against African American voters.

The Assembly, however, turned down Brent's request for the vote. Even though she was denied the right to vote, the General Assembly said that she could continue to represent the Calvert estate in Maryland. After a disagreement with Cecil Calvert, however, Margaret Brent finally decided to leave Maryland and moved to Virginia, where she successfully ran her own plantation until she died in 1671.

Responsibility in Action

Maryland's students learn about the importance of voting. In the state's *We the People . . . The Citizen and the Constitution Program,* students study voting rights. With your teacher, do research to find out how people in Maryland register to vote. Then make a guide about voter registration and share it with your parents and neighbors.

113

Maryland and China

People in the state of Maryland and in the country of China are citizens. In both places, people can participate in their local governments.

You have learned that in Maryland people vote to elect government leaders. Marylanders decide who they want to lead them. Citizens in Maryland can also voice their opinions and work for change if they are unhappy with their government's actions.

NORTH AMERICA **EUROPE** **ASIA**
MARYLAND
ATLANTIC OCEAN **CHINA**
AFRICA **PACIFIC OCEAN**
PACIFIC OCEAN **SOUTH AMERICA** **N** **INDIAN OCEAN** **AUSTRALIA**
0 — 2,000 Miles
0 — 2,000 Kilometers
ANTARCTICA

▶ **Before a general election, state candidates campaign with signs that ask people to vote for them.**

Tim **Cooney**
DELEGATE
DISTRICT 15

GARR

ABRAMS
COUNTY EXECUTIVE

MARK SHRI

ALAN CHEUNG
A FAN OF EDUCATION
Board of Education

RE-ELECT
LEVITAN
TO THE STATE SENATE

KEEP
Betty Ann
KRAHNKE

PHIL ANDRE
COUNTY COUN

JEAN **ROESS**
FOR STATE SENAT

HOUSE of DELEGATES (D-15)
Burt GOLDS

MARY OERGERS
DEMOCRAT GOVERNOR

COUNCIL RICT 1

FICKER
FOR DELEGATE
LOWER TAXES!

Maryland's voters listen to candidates and then vote for their choices on Election Day.

114

In China the Communist Party controls the government. It decides who will be a candidate for the National People's Congress. The Communist Party also chooses the country's highest leader, who then writes laws and appoints judges.

The people of China participate in local meetings. In some villages, people are beginning to elect their own town leaders.

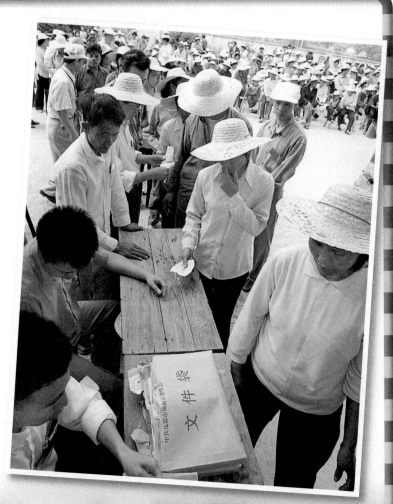

▶ The Chinese people vote in local elections, but candidates may not disagree with the Communist party.

▶ Today in China, local elections are sometimes held, even though the law says that local Communist party officials should appoint local officials.

Suburbs or Farmland?

As the population grows, people are moving into areas that used to be farmland. This trend is the subject of a heated debate.

The debate over how we should use our land is as old as the nation itself. Two founders of the United States, Alexander Hamilton and Thomas Jefferson, had different ideas about it too. Jefferson thought that we should be a nation of farmers. Alexander Hamilton believed in building great cities that would be centers of trade and manufacturing.

In 1791, as a member of President George Washington's cabinet, Alexander Hamilton argued for tariffs to protect American companies. A tariff is a special tax put on goods that are made outside the country. Hamilton believed a tariff would encourage the growth of factories and cities. This growth would mean that more land would be used for manufacturing and transportation. Thomas Jefferson thought that America's greatest strength was in its farms, so he was opposed to this tariff.

Today some people still worry about the spread of suburbs. They argue that building more suburbs leads to more pollution. People in suburbs need to drive longer distances to get to work. Those who are against building more suburbs think that new houses should be built in cities. They want to pass laws that limit growth in the countryside.

Others say that building neighborhoods in the country gives people more space and quieter neighborhoods. They think crowded cities will become even more polluted from traffic jams.

One solution may be something called "brownfields" development. Brownfields are areas within cities that once held old factories or other buildings. Some people say that these empty brownfields should be cleaned up and used for new homes. The U.S. government supports brownfield development as an alternative to sprawling cities and suburbs.

"*Manufacture must therefore be resorted to of necessity not of choice. . . . Those who labor in the earth are the chosen people. . . .*"

Thomas Jefferson, *Notes on the State of Virginia, 1781–1784*

"*Not only the wealth, but the independence and security of a Country, appear to be . . . connected with the prosperity of manufactures.*"

Alexander Hamilton, *Report on Manufactures, 1791*

"*Nothing we do will mean more to our children and to our future generations.*"

Parris Glendening, *former Maryland governor, writing about Maryland's Smart Growth Campaign, 2002*

Issues and You

People who support limits on growth say that these actions will be better for the environment. They also say it will revive the cities. People on the other side say that limits on growth take away people's freedom to choose. Do some research in the library or on the Internet to learn more about this issue. Then write a letter to your local officials explaining whether you are for or against laws that limit growth.

MARYLAND

Hagerstown
Baltimore

PREVIEW

Focus on the Main Idea
Citizens of Maryland celebrate their diverse ethnic and cultural backgrounds.

PLACES
Baltimore
Hagerstown

PEOPLE
Benjamin Banneker
Frederick Douglass
Matthew Henson
Eubie Blake
Billie Holiday

VOCABULARY
diversity

TERM
population density

EVENTS
Showcase of Nations
Celtic Festival of Southern Maryland

▶ People from many nations call Maryland home.

Maryland's Diverse People

You Are There When the music stops, everyone jumps up clapping. You and your friend, Kadir, join in with loud whistles. Wow! What an exciting dance by El Teatro de Danza Contemporañea de El Salvador (el tay AH troh day DAN sa kon tem por RAH nay ah day el SAHL vah dor).

"Isn't Artscape a fun festival?" Kadir smiles. Kadir had moved to Baltimore from Turkey, a country in the Middle East.

"There are people from so many places in Baltimore," he says.

"Kadir, this performance is only the beginning! Next, we'll hear African drumming and then see Irish dancers."

But first, let's have a bratwurst sandwich!

Main Idea and Details As you read, look for details that show how Marylanders celebrate their diverse ethnic and cultural backgrounds.

Maryland's Population

More than five million people live in Maryland. That is a lot of people for such a small state!

The **population density** in Maryland is one of the country's highest. Population density is the average number of people living on a measured area of land, such as a square mile. When many people live within a square mile as they do in a big city, the population density is high. When few people live within a square mile, the population density is low. Another way to measure population is to show how many people live in an area. The map below shows about how many people live in each Maryland county.

Most Marylanders live in cities or suburbs. **Baltimore,** Maryland's most populated city, has about 651,000 people. About one-third of the state's people live in the suburbs near Washington, D.C. Others live in Maryland cities west of Chesapeake Bay, such as Gaithersburg or Cumberland.

About one sixth of Maryland's people live in rural areas, mostly in the western and southern parts of the state and along the eastern shore of Chesapeake Bay.

REVIEW How does Maryland's size affect its population? *Cause and Effect*

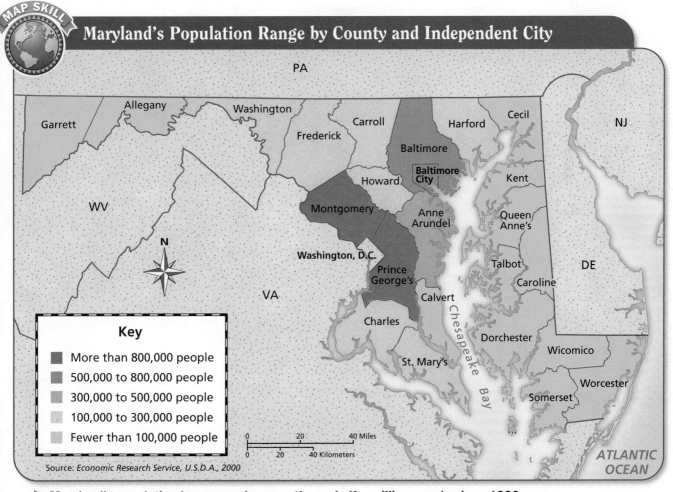

MAP SKILL

Maryland's Population Range by County and Independent City

Key
- ■ More than 800,000 people
- ■ 500,000 to 800,000 people
- ■ 300,000 to 500,000 people
- ■ 100,000 to 300,000 people
- ■ Fewer than 100,000 people

Source: *Economic Research Service, U.S.D.A., 2000*

▶ Maryland's population has grown by more than a half a million people since 1990.

MAP SKILL Understand Population *Which two counties are in the highest population range?*

Ethnic Groups

You have read that Maryland was founded on religious tolerance. From the beginning, Maryland has been a place where people of all religions and cultures are welcomed.

During the 1800s the Port of Baltimore was the second largest entry point for immigrants coming into the United States. Maryland became the home of people from many different religions and ethnic or racial backgrounds. Baltimore attracted a great **diversity,** or variety, of immigrants.

Today, Maryland is still the home of many ethnic groups. People from as many as 145 of the world's countries live in the state. Since 1990 many thousands of new immigrants have settled in Maryland.

At first many new immigrants in Maryland live in neighborhoods with other immigrants from the same country. Living near people from the same country makes it possible for groups to keep their native language, foods, and cultural traditions. Maryland's immigrants are able to enrich our state and the United States with their cultural traditions.

▶ **Maryland's schools enjoy the ethnic diversity of students from many cultural heritages.**

► Ethnic festivals in Maryland are sometimes held during the summer. This dancer can help visitors learn about Native American culture.

Many Latinos, or Latin Americans, also call Maryland their home. They have come to Maryland from Puerto Rico, Mexico, and El Salvador. Latinos bring their own unique cultures to Maryland.

Asian Americans from countries as far away as China and Japan live in Maryland. Others come from India and Pakistan. Some groups create community centers where they can celebrate similar cultural traditions together.

Many immigrants from Europe bring European culture to Maryland. People from Poland, Italy, Greece, Ireland, and Russia add diversity to the state.

Maryland's Amish people have roots in Switzerland. They choose to live simple, rural lives and often travel by horse-drawn vehicles. Some back roads of southern Maryland are lined with well-kept Amish farms.

A few thousand Native Americans live in Maryland. They are from Native American groups such as the Piscataway and Pocomoke. Native Americans sometimes celebrate their heritage at powwows featuring dancers and ceremonies.

Throughout Maryland, diverse ethnic groups share their cultures through restaurants, museums, concerts, and festivals. Marylanders of many ethnic backgrounds can enjoy and learn from rich cultural differences.

These neighborhoods and communities in Baltimore give the city its reputation as being a "City of Neighborhoods." Here, everyone can enjoy diverse cultures.

Many African Americans were first brought to Maryland as enslaved people. Others immigrated on their own. African Americans celebrate different traditions such as drumming, story telling, music, and dance.

REVIEW Summarize the ways that Marylanders share their ethnic diversity.
🕄 Summarize

Maryland's African American Heritage

You have read that the first African Americans came to Maryland to work as free people, servants, or slaves. Enslaved people worked without rights or property. When slavery ended after the Civil War, some African Americans chose to leave Maryland. Others stayed, however, and were joined by immigrants from several African nations.

Throughout history, African Americans have contributed to Maryland in important ways. Their life stories are celebrated in many of Maryland's museums.

The Banneker-Douglass Museum in Annapolis is named for Benjamin Banneker and Frederick Douglass. Benjamin Banneker was an African American inventor and astronomer.

▶ The United States Postal Service honored Benjamin Banneker by placing his portrait on this stamp.

HARPER'S WEEKLY.
JOURNAL OF CIVILIZATION.
Vol. XXVII.—No. 1405.   NEW YORK, SATURDAY, NOVEMBER 24, 1883.   TEN CENTS A COPY. WITH A SUPPLEMENT.

▶ Frederick Douglass wrote about his experiences and helped people understand the hardships of enslaved people.

Benjamin Banneker

Black Heritage USA 15c

He also helped survey the federal territory where Washington, D.C. was built. Although Banneker's grandmother had taught him to read, Banneker taught himself about mathematics and science.

Frederick Douglass became famous for his efforts to end slavery. The museum that shares his name has one of the country's largest collections of African American artifacts and art.

Baltimore's Great Blacks in Wax Museum has more than 100 life-sized wax figures of famous African Americans. Eighteen of them are Marylanders, including Thurgood Marshall and Matthew Henson. Henson was part of the expedition believed to be the first to reach the North Pole.

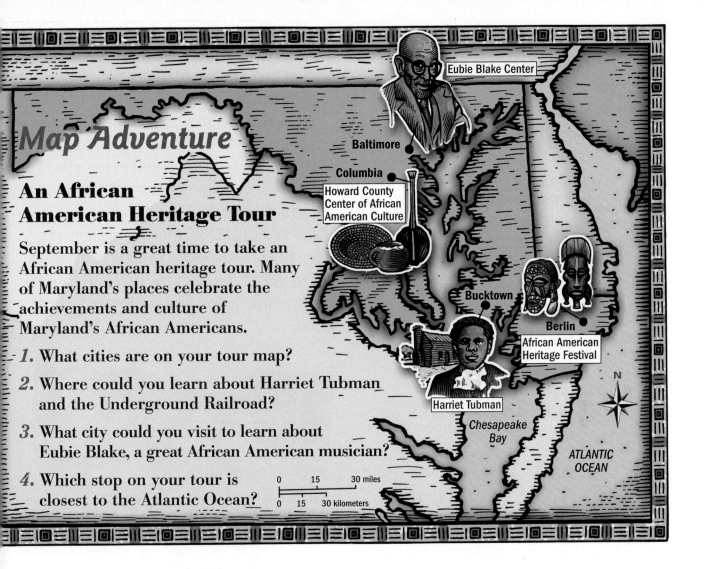

Map Adventure

An African American Heritage Tour

September is a great time to take an African American heritage tour. Many of Maryland's places celebrate the achievements and culture of Maryland's African Americans.

1. What cities are on your tour map?

2. Where could you learn about Harriet Tubman and the Underground Railroad?

3. What city could you visit to learn about Eubie Blake, a great African American musician?

4. Which stop on your tour is closest to the Atlantic Ocean?

Eubie Blake Center

Baltimore

Columbia

Howard County Center of African American Culture

Bucktown

Berlin

African American Heritage Festival

Harriet Tubman

Chesapeake Bay

ATLANTIC OCEAN

N

0   15   30 miles
0   15   30 kilometers

Billie Holiday and Eubie Blake, two of Maryland's great African American musicians, are also honored in the museum. **Eubie Blake** was a talented musician and composer of ragtime music. **Billie Holiday** is celebrated as one of America's greatest female jazz and blues singers. On Baltimore's Pennsylvania Avenue, you can see a sculpture of Billie Holiday.

Maryland's African American visual artists create paintings, sculptures, and other art forms. Joshua Johnston was a nationally recognized African American portrait painter. Portraits that he painted between 1796 and 1824 are displayed at the Maryland Historical Society. Nathaniel Gibbs is also a well-known painter.

REVIEW Summarize the ways African Americans have contributed to Maryland.
⟲ **Summarize**

▶ **Nathaniel Gibbs is a contemporary African American artist whose paintings often recreate Civil War scenes.**

Honoring Diversity

Marylanders honor their diversity throughout the year with a variety of ethnic festivals. You can enjoy food, music, dance, crafts, and games from many countries at these events.

Throughout the summer, Baltimore offers a series of festivals called the **Showcase of Nations.** Thousands of people come to celebrate the heritage of people from Poland, African countries, Latin American countries, Germany, Ukraine, Ireland, Greece, and Korea.

Each festival offers something unique. The Latin festival features dancers in colorful costumes. The Korean festival offers martial arts demonstrations. And storytellers bring Polish legends alive at a Polish festival. If steel drums and beautiful costumes are of interest, you might want to visit the Caribbean Carnival and Festival. Ethnic festivals such as these provide weekend entertainment throughout the summer and early fall for Marylanders and visitors to our state.

FACT FILE

Maryland's Ethnic Festivals

One way in which Maryland celebrates its ethnic diversity is with festivals. In Baltimore, the Showcase of Nations festivals run from May through October.

▶ LatinoFest, one of Baltimore's Showcase of Nations festivals, is filled with music, dancing, and delicious foods.

▶ At the oldest Celtic Festival, in St. Leonard, Maryland, you can hear bagpipers, drummers, and fiddlers play rousing tunes for many dance performances.

▶ Asian American martial arts demonstrations are fun to watch at Baltimore's Korean Festival.

Hagerstown, Maryland, celebrates each August with a German festival. Augustoberfest honors Hagerstown's relationship with Wesel, Germany, its sister city. Activities include a Friday night concert and family activities on Saturday. Festival guests can sample German food and enjoy programs for adults and children.

The **Celtic Festival of Southern Maryland** is an exciting yearly event in St. Leonard. The town comes alive with athletic competitions and the sound of bagpipes and fiddling from Scotland, Ireland, and Wales.

Marylanders also honor their diversity with ethnic film festivals, art exhibits, concerts, and classes. These events offer a special look into the lives and cultures of Maryland's diverse people.

REVIEW Summarize the ways Marylanders express their ethnic diversity.
⤻ Summarize

Summarize the Lesson

- **Maryland has a growing population.**
- **People from many different ethnic backgrounds live in Maryland.**
- **Throughout Maryland's history, African Americans have contributed to the economy and culture of the state.**
- **Marylanders find many ways to honor and celebrate their ethnic diversity.**

LESSON 3 REVIEW

Check Facts and Main Ideas

1. **Main Idea and Details** On a separate sheet of paper, fill in the graphic organizer with four ways that citizens of Maryland celebrate their diverse ethnic and cultural backgrounds.

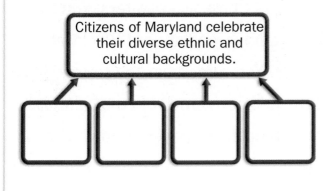

Citizens of Maryland celebrate their diverse ethnic and cultural backgrounds.

2. Where do most of Maryland's people live?

3. What about Maryland's history has made it a place for people from around the world to settle?

4. Name some contributions to the culture of Maryland and the United States made by people from different cultural groups.

5. **Critical Thinking: *Draw Conclusions*** How does the population range in Garrett County differ from the population range in Prince George's County, and why do you think they are so different?

Link to ⚭ **Art**

Create a Festival Poster Use your creative ideas to make a poster for the Maryland ethnic festival of your choice. Make sure to design your poster so it appeals to students in your age group.

Friendsville

MARYLAND

Deal Island

PREVIEW

Focus on the Main Idea
Marylanders celebrate their state and its regional traditions.

PLACES
Deal Island
Friendsville

PEOPLE
Barbara Fritchie

VOCABULARY
decoy
artisan

TERM
crab pots

EVENTS
Preakness® Stakes
Ward Museum World
  Championship Wildfowl
  Carving Competition

My Poetry Journal

Marylanders Celebrate Their State

You Are There

"Just stick with it. You can do it!" says your mother smiling.

"I know, Mom, but I really want to do a good a job to win the Maryland Day poetry contest our class is having. I want to remember the beautiful things I saw on our Eastern Shore vacation last year to help me think of what to write."

You close your eyes and see white skipjack sails on glittering Chesapeake waters. You hear birds in the swampy woodlands of Blackwater Wildlife Refuge. You remember the sound of waves and the delicious smell of crab cakes in Ocean City. You open your eyes, grab your pen, and begin to write.

"Once on a Maryland summer day . . ." Writing a poem to celebrate Maryland will be easy!

Main Idea and Details As you read, notice details that show how Marylanders celebrate their state and its regional traditions.

Celebrating Our State Heritage

Marylanders honor their state with special events, state symbols, and literature. One event that Marylanders celebrate is Maryland Day. Each year Marylanders look forward to March 25, an official state holiday. It marks the day in 1634 when settlers from Europe stepped off the *Ark* and the *Dove* to make a new home in Maryland. To celebrate, special events are held all around the state.

You do not have to be a Marylander to enjoy many of the state's other events. The famous **Preakness® Stakes** brings tourists to Maryland from all over the world. The Preakness® is a week-long celebration in Baltimore during which Marylanders honor not only their horseracing tradition but also hold hot-air balloon races, parades, and concerts.

▶ Balloons race as part of the Preakness® Stakes celebration.

Barbara Fritchie
by *John Greenleaf Whittier*

This excerpt from Whittier's poem celebrates Fritchie's patriotism.

....

Up the street came the rebel tread,
Stonewall Jackson riding ahead.

Under his slouched hat left and right
He glanced; the old flag met his sight.

"Halt!" the dust-brown ranks stood fast.
"Fire!" out blazed the rifle-blast.

It shivered the window, pane and sash;
It rent the banner with seam and gash.

Quick, as it fell, from the broken staff
Dame Barbara snatched the silken scarf.

She leaned far out on the window-sill,
And shook it forth with a royal will.

"Shoot, if you must, this old gray head,
But spare your country's flag," she said.

Maryland celebrates with its state symbols too. A 400-pound stained-glass sculpture of a blue crab greets visitors at the Baltimore airport. It reminds Marylanders and visitors to Maryland of Chesapeake Bay's rich resources.

Marylanders also celebrate their heritage with storytelling. Poet John Greenleaf Whittier told the story of brave **Barbara Fritchie.** The story, above, says that her patriotism protected the town of Frederick from being attacked during the Civil War.

REVIEW Summarize the different ways in which Marylanders celebrate their state heritage. ⊃ **Summarize**

127

Regional Traditions

You have read about Maryland's three regions and how each one is special. Marylanders living in the Atlantic Coastal Plain region, the Piedmont Plateau region, and the Appalachian Mountain region carry on many historic traditions.

One part of the Atlantic Coastal Plain is the Eastern Shore. A lifetime resident described the Eastern Shore as "slow-paced and community-oriented." She said, "The residents like to learn about the history and preserve it."

Each year at the end of summer, Marylanders in this region celebrate the tradition of the skipjack watermen at the annual Skipjack Races and Land Festival on **Deal Island.** The watermen race their skipjacks, one of Maryland's state symbols, on a ten-mile course shaped like a triangle.

As one of Maryland's many fishers, Gladston Tyler knows all about skipjack boats. Tyler is a waterman from Smith Island who carries on the fishing tradition. Before dawn, Tyler swings his boat into Chesapeake Bay for a day of crabbing. He searches in the early morning light for his **crab pots,** or traps for catching crabs. Tyler checks about 400 crab pots each day during the crabbing season. On a good day, each pot will hold a dozen or more crabs. That is nearly 5,000 crabs!

Tyler and other watermen know the bay well after generations of crabbing. One legend says that during a thick fog, watermen can figure out where they are simply by smelling a handful of mud from the shallow bottom of the bay.

After a day of fishing, many watermen enjoy their state's special dish, crab cakes. These delicious patties made of crabmeat, bread crumbs, mayonnaise, and seasonings are a world-famous Maryland tradition.

▶ **The watermen and their skipjack boats are an Eastern Shore tradition.**

▶ The Chesapeake and Ohio Canal near Great Falls attracts tourists to Maryland.

Marylanders in the Piedmont Plateau region celebrate another delicious tradition. Each year at the end of winter, the people of Westminster welcome visitors to the Maple Sugarin' Festival. Participants help tap the trees, collect the sticky sap in a bucket, boil down the sap, and finally taste the sweet syrup at a pancake breakfast. The festival is just one way people in the Piedmont Plateau celebrate their regional traditions.

You have also read about the C&O Canal in the Appalachian Mountain region and how it gave Marylanders a new way to travel. Today, western Marylanders celebrate their region's heritage and keep the tradition of canal travel alive. Canal Place in Cumberland is dedicated to this tradition. At Canal Place, tourists might climb aboard a canal boat replica with a costumed tour guide. In spring many visitors enter youth-only contests to win prizes during CanalFest! Each year, Canal Place adds more activities and events to carry on the canal traditions of the Appalachian Mountain region.

REVIEW What Atlantic Coastal Plain traditions grew from the region's closeness to waterways?
Cause and Effect

▶ Each year maple trees in the Piedmont Plateau region produce sap for making delicious maple syrup.

Celebrating with Music and Crafts

Marylanders also celebrate their heritage and traditions with music and crafts. Each region is known for its own style of music or type of craft.

The marshes of the Atlantic Coastal Plain, for example, attract a variety of ducks. Hunters lure the ducks using **decoys,** or carved wooden statues. Sometimes carvers create such beautiful decoys that no one wants to put the carvings into the water. In Ocean City the **Ward Museum World Championship Wildfowl Carving Competition** gives master carvers the chance to display and celebrate their art.

The Piedmont Plateau celebrates a more historic craft. **Artisans,** or skilled craftsworkers, at the Carroll County Farm Museum demonstrate how families performed their daily activities long ago. These activities included spinning and weaving their own fabric for clothing. Artisans also demonstrate basket weaving, blacksmithing, rug hooking, and candle and soap making.

Children visiting the farm museum can celebrate these crafts hands-on. The artisans teach children how to make cloth, candles, and soap. Children can even play with the same kinds of handcrafted toys that Maryland children played with in the 1880s.

In the Appalachian Mountain region, songs that are hundreds of years old are still sung today. Musicians tell old and new stories while playing guitars, banjos, and dulcimers, which are traditional stringed instruments.

Marylanders keep mountain music alive with events like the Fiddle and Banjo Contest in **Friendsville.** Musicians as young as seven years old enter the contest! Few visitors can resist joining in the lively folk dances once the music starts.

▶ Mountain music brings thousands of tourists to western Maryland each year.

Another popular event is the Rocky Gap Country/Bluegrass Music Festival in Cumberland. More than 10,000 people attend the festival each year! The weekend event features concerts, music workshops, and sing-alongs that celebrate the music of the Appalachian Mountain region.

REVIEW In what ways do Marylanders from the Appalachian Mountain region use music to celebrate their traditions? Main Idea and Details

▶ Visitors at the Carroll County Farm Museum learn about crafts that were important to Marylanders in the 1800s, such as basket weaving.

Summarize the Lesson

- Marylanders celebrate their state's heritage with special events, state symbols, and literature.

- Each of the three regions of Maryland has its own traditions.

- People in Maryland celebrate with regional music and crafts.

LESSON 4 REVIEW

Check Facts and Main Ideas

1. Main Idea and Details On a separate sheet of paper, complete the diagram with details that show the ways that Marylanders celebrate their state and its regional traditions.

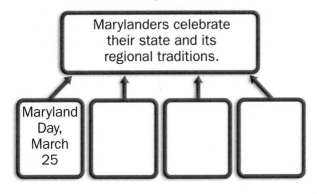

Marylanders celebrate their state and its regional traditions.

Maryland Day, March 25

2. What are two of Maryland's state symbols?

3. How do people in the Atlantic Coastal Plain region celebrate their traditions?

4. In what ways do people in the Piedmont Plateau region and the Appalachian Mountain region celebrate their traditions?

5. Critical Thinking: *Cause and Effect* In what ways are Maryland's historical sites related to recreational activities in the state?

Link to ⊶ Writing

Write a Newspaper Story Use books and the Internet to learn about a festival in one of Maryland's three regions. Write a short newspaper story telling readers what the event is about.

LESSON 5

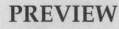

MARYLAND

Havre de Grace•

PREVIEW

Focus on the Main Idea
Marylanders find many ways to have fun in their state.

PLACE
Havre de Grace

PEOPLE
Charles Willson Peale
Cal Ripken, Jr.
Johnny Unitas
Tom Clancy
Anne Tyler

VOCABULARY
jousting
lacrosse

▶ After graduating from high school in 1978, Cal Ripken, Jr., joined the Baltimore Orioles.

Recreation in Maryland

You Are There

2001 is such an exciting year for baseball!

"Hurry up! We don't want you to get lost in the crowd." Your uncle leads you through the fans. How exciting!

This sports writing job is your first for the school newspaper. Here you are at Camden Yard on October 6 to watch the Baltimore Orioles play the Boston Red Sox. But this game isn't just any baseball game. Today is the last game for Orioles' Cal Ripken, Jr. He played with the Baltimore Orioles for twenty years!

You slide into your seat just in time to see him introduced. The crowd yells out Cal's name. Your uncle reminds you to get out your notebook. Play ball!

Summarize As you read, notice the sports and other activities that Marylanders enjoy.

Maryland's Artists

Many Marylanders enjoy the arts. Some create paintings and sculptures. Others enjoy the works that Maryland's artists have created.

Marylander **Charles Willson Peale** was one of the leading portrait artists of his time. Born in Queen Anne's County in 1741, Peale was the first artist to paint a portrait of George Washington and other Revolutionary War figures. He became well known as the "Artist of the American Revolution." Peale started what is now the oldest art school in the country, the Pennsylvania Academy of Fine Arts.

The Maryland Commission on Artistic Property has collected 11 of Peale's historic paintings, including *Washington, Lafayette and Tilghman at Yorktown,* and a portrait of William Paca.

Baltimore sculptor Reuben Kramer is famous for his huge bronze sculpture of Supreme Court Justice Thurgood Marshall. The statue stands outside the U.S. courthouse in Baltimore.

"When I was a child in east Baltimore," Kramer said, "I was always building things out of scraps—tin, leather, wood, et cetera—picked up from nearby factories."

By the time he was in his teens, Kramer was making sculptures. During his long career, he was especially interested in promoting civil rights. In 1944 he helped start and then directed the first

► Charles Willson Peale was a well-known painter from Maryland.

racially integrated art school to be registered in Maryland. He continued to win awards for his work during a 70-year career. Kramer lived and worked in Baltimore until his death in 1999. He was 89 years old.

REVIEW What helped make Charles Willson Peale and Reuben Kramer important artists in Maryland? **Main Idea and Details**

► Reuben Kramer was well-known for his interest in civil rights, which may have inspired his statue of Thurgood Marshall.

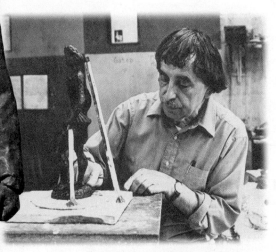

► Reuben Kramer creates a statue in his studio.

133

Sports in Maryland

Many Marylanders enjoy a variety of sports. You may be familiar with most of these sports. Some well-known professional teams, such as the Baltimore Orioles baseball team and the Baltimore Ravens of the National Football League, call Maryland home. The Baltimore Burn of the National Women's Football League and nine other teams began playing in April of 2001. The Washington Redskins of the National Football League play in Landover, Maryland. College teams, such as the University of Maryland Terps basketball team, also draw a lot of fans. Minor league baseball teams—the Bowie Baysox, the Delmarva Shorebirds, the Frederick Keys, and the Hagerstown Suns—also have loyal local fans.

Other sports, like jousting, may be new to you. **Jousting** is a sport in which players race on horses down a track. They try to capture three rings on long spears called lances. Jousting originated long ago in Europe. Two lance-carrying armored knights charged at each other, each trying

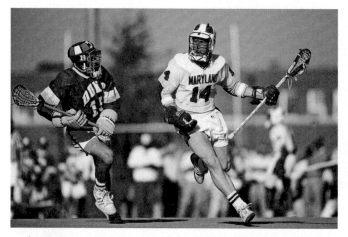

▶ Jousting competitions are a popular Maryland activity.

to knock the other off his horse. Today jousting is not as dangerous. Popular since colonial times, Maryland adopted jousting as its state sport in 1962. Today Marylanders of all ages can participate.

Marylanders also play **lacrosse,** the oldest team sport in North America.

▶ The lacrosse team at the University of Maryland is one of the best in the country.

Lacrosse players try to throw a rubber ball past a goalie and into a net, using a stick with a basket on the end of it. Each year, college lacrosse teams compete for the national championship. The Lacrosse Hall of Fame is located at Maryland's Johns Hopkins University.

You have also read that the Preakness® Stakes is a Maryland tradition. Marylanders take pride in preparing their horses for racing. Thoroughbred farms breed, train, exercise, groom, board, and give medical care to their prized horses. Trainers work very hard to make their horses the best racers at the Preakness®. Today nearly 100,000 people come to watch this famous sporting event.

You have read that many Marylanders enjoy playing sports. Born in Havre de Grace, Cal Ripken, Jr., was one of the best shortstops in baseball history. In 1998 his record-setting streak of playing in consecutive games ended at 2,632. That was 16 years without missing a game!

▶ Raising horses for racing is an old Maryland tradition that began when wealthy colonists went fox hunting.

Football hero Johnny Unitas led his team to victory in three championship games and one Super Bowl as quarterback for the Baltimore Colts. Although he was born in Pittsburgh, he earned his fame in Maryland. Unitas was the star quarterback for the Colts and is considered to be one of the greatest football players of all time.

REVIEW Briefly summarize some of Maryland's popular sporting events.
↻ **Summarize**

▶ Sporting events draw large numbers of fans in Maryland.

Maryland's Greats

Many famous and important people call Maryland home. Marylanders contribute to state and national politics, the arts, sports, science, and education. The variety of their achievements reflects the diversity of the state.

You have read that Billie Holiday was one of America's greatest jazz singers. Born in 1915, Holiday grew up in Baltimore. Listening to records by other musicians, she knew she wanted a singing career of her own. She began singing in New York jazz clubs. Her style was unique, and soon nearly everyone wanted to hear her and buy her records. Billie Holiday became one of Maryland's worldwide jazz legends.

Eubie Blake was born in 1883, and by the time he was six years old, he had already learned to play his family's pump organ. His career as a musical performer began at age 15.

Blake became a famous composer and performer of ragtime music and musical comedy during the 1920s. His career continued much longer, however. In 1969 he made an album called *The Eighty-six Years of Blake.* He had been a performer most of his life, and died just five days after his 100th birthday in February of 1983.

▶ **Billie Holiday was the most famous jazz singer of her time. People still buy her recordings today.**

▶ **Marylander Eubie Blake became a legend among fans of ragtime music.**

Famous authors call Maryland home, too. **Tom Clancy** is the author of many best-selling books about world politics. Maryland's location near Washington, D.C., puts Clancy in an ideal location to write about that topic. In 1997 a publisher signed a book contract with

▶ Readers can count on Tom Clancy for a suspenseful thriller about world politics.

▶ Anne Tyler won the Pulitzer Prize for her novel *Breathing Lessons.*

Clancy for more than $100 million. He became the highest paid author in the United States.

Many stories by author **Anne Tyler** take place in Baltimore. In 1989 one of her books won an important award called the Pulitzer Prize. Tyler's books deal with the lives of ordinary people. Anne Tyler and Tom Clancy help keep Maryland on the map as a state with great writers.

REVIEW Give a brief summary of Marylanders who became famous for their skill and creativity. ↻ Summarize

Summarize the Lesson

- **Marylanders enjoy many different kinds of sporting events.**
- **Maryland's famous sports heroes are a part of sports history.**
- **Maryland has produced famous achievers in music, literature, and art.**

LESSON 5 REVIEW

Check Facts and Main Ideas

1. ↻ Summarize On a separate sheet of paper, use the graphic organizer to help you organize details that will help summarize ways that Marylanders can have fun in their state.

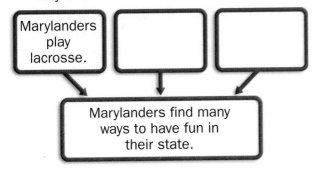

Marylanders play lacrosse.

Marylanders find many ways to have fun in their state.

2. What is Maryland's state sport?
3. Which Marylander set a record for the most consecutive baseball games played?
4. Who are some of Maryland's most famous writers and musicians?
5. **Critical Thinking:** *Cause and Effect* How has Maryland's diverse cultural heritage contributed to activities that people enjoy in the state?

Link to ⚬⚬ **Writing**

Sports Report Choose your favorite Maryland sport and write a report about a real or fictional event in that sport for the school newspaper.

Chapter Summary

Summarize

On a sheet of paper, fill in the diagram to show how Maryland provides its people with opportunities for government participation and recreation. Then use the information to write a summary of opportunities for Marylanders.

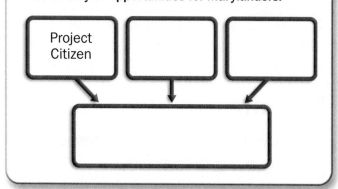

Project Citizen

Main Ideas and Skills

1 Main Idea How do Marylanders participate in politics as citizens?

2 Main Idea What services do Maryland's state and local governments provide for their citizens?

3 Main Idea What are some ways that Marylanders celebrate their diverse ethnic backgrounds?

4 Main Idea Why are the activities in each of Maryland's regions different from those of other regions of the state?

5 Main Idea Name some of Maryland's famous literary figures.

6 Critical Thinking: *Cause and Effect* How does citizen participation make Maryland a better place to live?

Apply Skills

7 Understand a Flowchart According to the flowchart on page 104, what happens to a bill that is introduced in one house, but is not approved in the other house?

Vocabulary and Places

Match each word with a correct definition or description.

1 bill (p. 95)

2 ballot (p. 108)

3 diversity (p. 120)

4 artisan (p. 130)

5 jousting (p. 134)

a. skilled craftsworker

b. a game on horseback and Maryland's state sport

c. variety

d. a way of casting a secret vote

e. a proposed new law

Write a sentence about each of the following places. You may use two or more in a single sentence.

6 Baltimore (p. 93)

7 Harford County (p. 107)

8 Hagerstown (p. 125)

9 Deal Island (p. 128)

10 Havre de Grace (p. 135)

Write About Maryland

1 Write a poem about Maryland that you could enter in a Maryland Day contest.

2 Write a tribute about a famous person from Maryland, giving details about his or her achievements and contributions to the state.

3 Write a letter to a Maryland state leader describing a problem in your community, and a proposed solution.

End with a Song

Maryland, My Maryland

"Maryland, My Maryland" was adopted as the official state song in 1939. The words were first written as a poem and then set to the music of "O, Tannenbaum" (also called "Oh, Christmas Tree").

Words by James Ryder Randall

Traditional

1. The des-pot's heel is on thy shore, Mar - y-land, my

Mar - y-land! His torch is at thy tem - ple door,

Mar - y-land, my Mar - y-land! A - venge the pat - ri -

ot - ic gore that flecked the streets of Bal - ti-more, and

be the bat - tle queen of yore, Mar - y-land, my Mar - y-land!

Unit Review

Main Ideas and Vocabulary

Read the passage below and use it to answer the questions that follow.

Maryland has many varied landforms and three different regions. The Appalachian Mountain region is ideal for mining resources such as coal and natural gas. Canals and railroads built there years ago provided Marylanders with better transportation.

At the foot of the mountains, the Piedmont Plateau region provides Maryland with plenty of fertile soil. Farmers grow crops there such as soybeans, corn, vegetables, and wheat. They also raise dairy cows and chickens.

The Atlantic Coastal Plain region surrounds Chesapeake Bay. Its water resources provide Marylanders with food and opportunities for jobs and recreation.

Marylanders in each region celebrate with unique festivals and traditions. The Appalachian Mountain region celebrates with mountain music contests. The Piedmont Plateau region attracts many visitors with its artisans who demonstrate skills and crafts at the Carroll County Farm Museum. The Atlantic Coastal Plain draws crowds with skipjack races and the Preakness® Stakes horse race. Each region has a special way to celebrate its traditions.

1 The main idea of this passage is that
   A crowds attend the Preakness® horse race.
   B Maryland has three unique regions.
   C Chesapeake Bay provides opportunities for jobs and recreation.
   D Maryland's regions celebrate with festivals.

2 In this passage the word *Piedmont* probably means
   A the mountain region.
   B at the foot of the mountain.
   C river valley.
   D swamp.

3 Why are so many crops grown in the Piedmont Plateau region?
   A The region has fertile soil.
   B The region's farm museum attracts visitors with crafts.
   C Farmers there raise cattle and chickens.
   D The region has a high-altitude climate.

4 In this passage the word *artisans* means
   A skilled craftsworkers.
   B watermen.
   C farmers.
   D attractions.

People and Terms

Match each person or term to its description.

1. **coastal plain** (p. 14)
2. **Giovanni Verrazano** (p. 52)
3. **Stamp Act** (p. 59)
4. **Mary Pickersgill** (p. 67)
5. **Thurgood Marshall** (p. 99)
6. **Billie Holiday** (p. 123)

a. served on the U.S. Supreme Court

b. female jazz singer

c. unpopular British tax on colonies

d. first European explorer to sail through Chesapeake Bay

e. low, flat land near an ocean

f. made a famous U.S. battle flag

Apply Skills

Make a Circle Graph You are helping your family plan a trip in Maryland. You will have 10 days to visit three Maryland cities: Baltimore, Annapolis, and Hagerstown. You will need about 2.5 days, or 25% of your time for travel. That is one-fourth of the circle. The other 75%, or three-fourths, of the time is yours to spend in the three cities. How much time will you spend in each city? That is up to you! Remember that the circle represents 100% of the time that you have, or 10 days. The 2.5 days of travel time will be one "slice" on the graph. You can divide the rest of the time any way you would like. To finish your circle graph, draw and label the "slices" of the graph to show what percentage of your time you will spend in each city.

Write and Share

Choose a person or place that is important to Maryland's geography, history, or culture. If you have chosen a person, write a short speech that tells who the person is, why he or she is important to Maryland, and why you chose this person. If you have chosen a place, write a short speech that tells where it is, why it is important to Maryland, and why it would be fun to visit there. Take turns giving your speeches to the class.

Read on Your Own

Look for these books in your library.

Reference Guide

Table of Contents

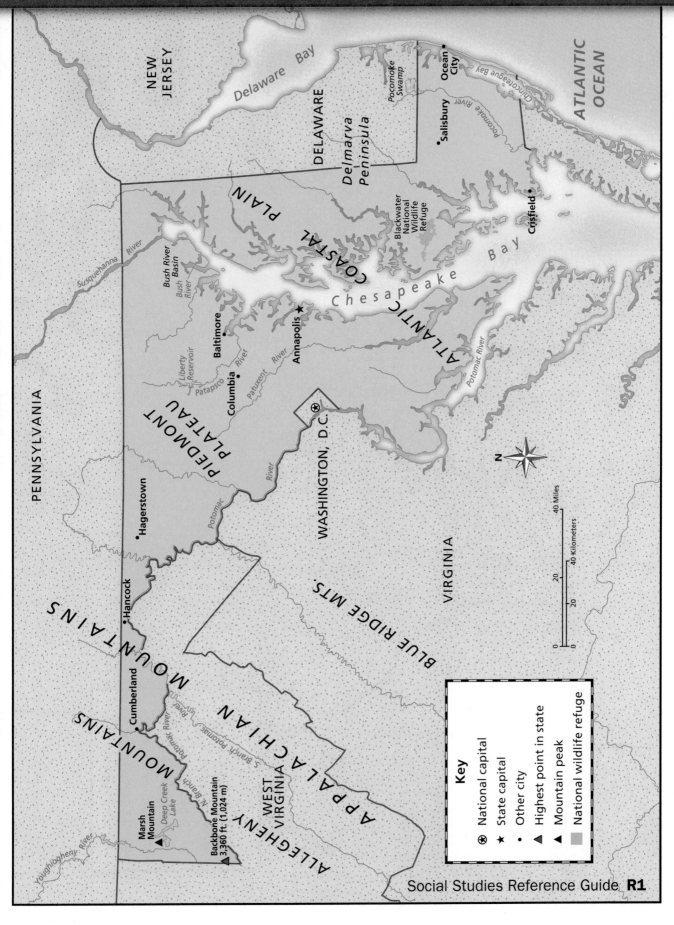

Key

⊛ National capital
★ State capital
• Other city
◣ Highest point in state
◣ Mountain peak
▨ National wildlife refuge

NEW JERSEY

Delaware Bay

DELAWARE

Pocomoke Swamp

Ocean City

Potomoke River

Chincoteague Bay

ATLANTIC OCEAN

Salisbury

Delmarva Peninsula

Blackwater National Wildlife Refuge

Crisfield

COASTAL PLAIN

Susquehanna River

Bush River Basin

Bush River

Chesapeake Bay

ATLANTIC

Baltimore

Liberty Reservoir

Patapsco River

Patuxent River

Columbia

Annapolis

River

WASHINGTON, D.C.

Potomac River

PENNSYLVANIA

PIEDMONT PLATEAU

Hagerstown

Potomac

River

N

40 Miles

40 Kilometers

20

20

Hancock

VIRGINIA

BLUE RIDGE MTS.

MOUNTAINS

Cumberland

N. Branch Potomac River

S. Branch Potomac River

APPALACHIAN

ALLEGHENY MOUNTAINS

WEST VIRGINIA

Marsh Mountain

Deep Creek Lake

N. Branch Potomac River

Youghiogheny River

◣ Backbone Mountain 3,360 ft. (1,024 m)

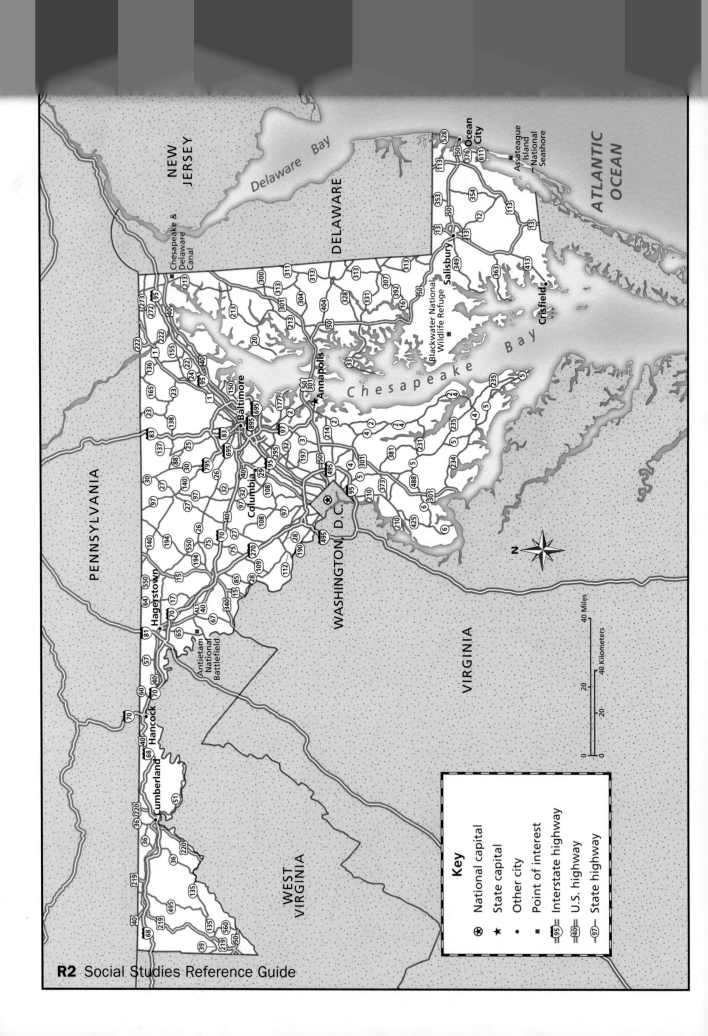

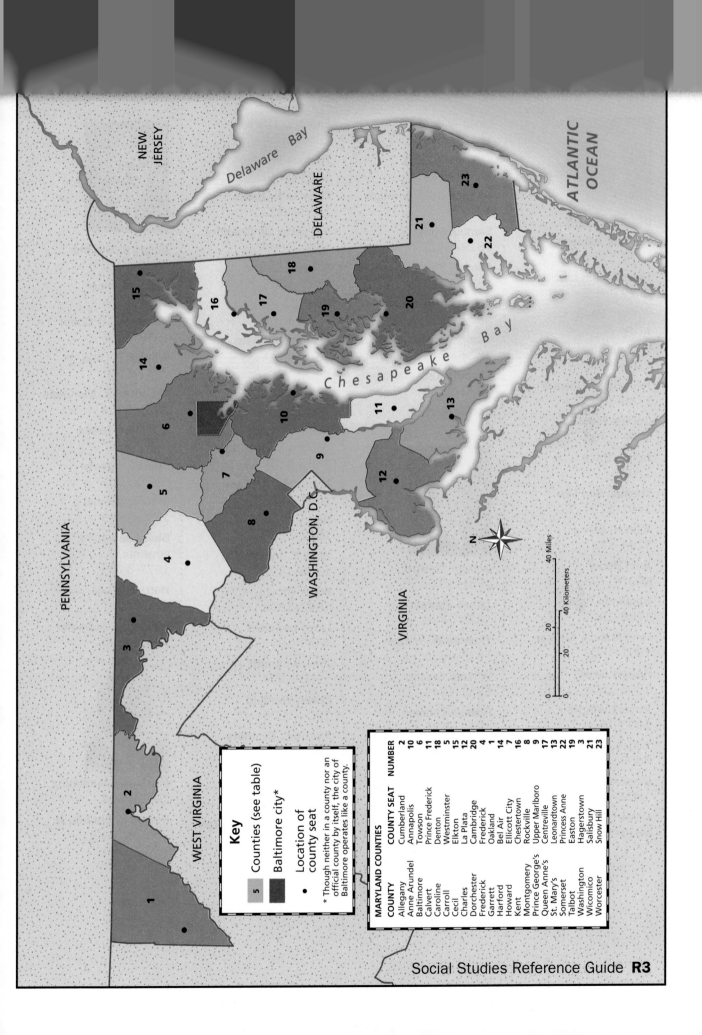

Key

Counties (see table)

5

Baltimore city*

• Location of county seat

* Though neither in a county nor an official county by itself, the city of Baltimore operates like a county.

MARYLAND COUNTIES

COUNTY	COUNTY SEAT	NUMBER
Allegany	Cumberland	2
Anne Arundel	Annapolis	10
Baltimore	Towson	6
Calvert	Prince Frederick	11
Caroline	Denton	18
Carroll	Westminster	5
Cecil	Elkton	15
Charles	La Plata	12
Dorchester	Cambridge	20
Frederick	Frederick	4
Garrett	Oakland	1
Harford	Bel Air	14
Howard	Ellicott City	7
Kent	Chestertown	16
Montgomery	Rockville	8
Prince George's	Upper Marlboro	9
Queen Anne's	Centreville	17
St. Mary's	Leonardtown	13
Somerset	Princess Anne	22
Talbot	Easton	19
Washington	Hagerstown	3
Wicomico	Salisbury	21
Worcester	Snow Hill	23

Thomas Johnson
1777–1779

Thomas Sim Lee
1779–1782

William Paca
1782–1785

William Smallwood
1785–1788

John Eager Howard
1788–1791

George Plater
1791–1792

James Brice
1792

Thomas Sim Lee
1792–1794

John H. Stone
1794–1797

John Henry
1797–1798

Benjamin Ogle
1798–1801

John Francis Mercer
1801–1803

Robert Bowie
1803–1806

Robert Wright
1806–1809

James Butcher
1809

Edward Lloyd
1809–1811

Robert Bowie
1811–1812

Levin Winder
1812–1816

Charles Ridgely
1816–1819

Charles Goldsborough
1819

Samuel Sprigg
1819–1822

Samuel Stevens, Jr.
1822–1826

Joseph Kent
1826–1829

Daniel Martin
1829–1830

Thomas King Carroll
1830–1831

Daniel Martin
1831

George Howard
1831–1833

James Thomas
1833–1836

Thomas W. Veazey
1836–1839

William Grason
1839–1842

Francis Thomas
1842–1845

Thomas G. Pratt
1845–1848

Philip Francis Thomas
1848–1851

Enoch L. Lowe
1851–1854

Thomas W. Ligon
1854–1858

Thomas H. Hicks
1858–1862

Augustus W. Bradford
1862–1866

Thomas Swann
1866–1869

Oden Bowie
1869–1872

William P. Whyte
1872–1874

James B. Groome
1874–1876

John Lee Carroll
1876–1880

William T. Hamilton
1880–1884

Robert M. McLane
1884–1885

Henry Lloyd
1885–1888

Elihu E. Jackson
1888–1892

Frank Brown
1892–1896

Lloyd Lowndes
1896–1900

John W. Smith
1900–1904

Edwin Warfield
1904–1908

Austin L. Crothers
1908–1912

Phillips L. Goldsborough
1912–1916

Emerson C. Harrington
1916–1920

Albert C. Ritchie
1920–1935

Harry W. Nice
1935–1939

Herbert R. O'Conor
1939–1947

William P. Lane, Jr.
1947–1951

Theodore R. McKeldin
1951–1959

J. Millard Tawes
1959–1967

Spiro T. Agnew
1967–1969

Marvin Mandel
1969–1979

Blair Lee (acting governor)
1977–1979

Harry Hughes
1979–1987

William D. Schaefer
1987–1995

Parris N. Glendening
1995–2003

Robert L. Ehrlich, Jr.
2003–present

Famous Marylanders

Spiro T. Agnew, Vice-President, Towson

George Armistead, commander of Fort McHenry

Benjamin Banneker, mathematician, astronomer, Ellicott

John Barth, writer, Cambridge

Clara Barton, founder of the American Red Cross, lived the end of her life in Glen Echo

Henry Blair, inventor, Montgomery County

Eubie Blake, musician, Baltimore

James M. Cain, writer, Annapolis

Charles Carroll, political leader, Annapolis

Rachel Carson, writer, scientist, lived much of her life in Maryland

Samuel Chase, political leader, jurist, Somerset County

Tom Clancy, writer, Baltimore

Dominique Dawes, Olympic gymnast, Silver Spring

Stephen Decatur, naval officer, Sinepuxent

John Dickinson, statesman, Talbot County

Frederick Douglass, abolitionist, editor, Tuckahoe

F. Scott Fitzgerald, writer, buried in Rockville

Christopher Gist, frontiersman, Baltimore

Philip Glass, composer, Baltimore

Robert Moses "Lefty" Grove, baseball player, Lonaconing

Dashiell Hammett, writer, St. Mary's County

John Hanson, senator, patriot, Charles County

Francis E. W. Harper, writer, educator, Baltimore

Matthew Alexander Henson, explorer, Charles County

Billie Holiday, singer, Baltimore

Johns Hopkins, financier, philanthropist, Anne Arundel County

John Eager Howard, soldier, governor, senator, Baltimore County

Reverdy Johnson, lawyer, statesman, Annapolis

Thomas Johnson, political leader, Calvert County

Thomas Kennedy, legislator, lived much of his life in Maryland

Francis Scott Key, lawyer, author, Carroll County

"Sugar" Ray Leonard, boxer, grew up in Palmer Park

Thurgood Marshall, jurist, civil rights advocate, Baltimore

Luther Martin, lawyer, political leader, Maryland attorney general 1778–1805

H. L. Mencken, writer, Baltimore

Ottmar Mergenthaler, inventor, lived much of his life in Baltimore

Kweisi Mfume, NAACP director, Baltimore

Ogden Nash, poet, lived much of his life in Baltimore

George Peabody, financier, philanthropist, Baltimore

Charles Willson Peale, painter, naturalist, Queen Anne's County

Mary Pickersgill, patriot, charity organizer, lived in Baltimore

Edgar Allan Poe, writer, lived several years in Baltimore

Emily Post, etiquette expert, Baltimore

Lizette Reese, poet, teacher, Waverly

Cal Ripken, Jr., baseball player, Havre de Grace

George Herman "Babe" Ruth, baseball player, Baltimore

Elizabeth Bayley Seton, religious leader, lived in Emmitsburg

Pam Shriver, tennis player, Baltimore

Sargent Shriver, public official, Westminster

Upton Sinclair, writer, Baltimore

Henrietta Szold, religious leader, Baltimore

Roger B. Taney, jurist, Calvert County

Harriet Tubman, abolitionist, Dorchester County

Anne Tyler, writer, lives in Maryland

Leon Uris, writer, Baltimore

Chick Webb, musician, Baltimore

Gazetteer

This gazetteer is a geographic dictionary that will help you locate and pronounce places in this book. It also gives the latitude and longitude for many places. The page numbers tell you where each place appears on a map (m.) or in the text (t.).

 A

Allegheny Mountains (al′ ə gā′ nē moun′ təns) Located in the western part of the Appalachian Mountain region and part of the Appalachian mountain system. (t. 18)

Annapolis (ə nap′ ə lis) Maryland's state capital, and site of the approval of the treaty for United States independence; Annapolis was the newly-formed nation's first capital; 39°N, 77°W. (t. 7, 62)

Antietam Creek (an tē′ təm krēk) Site of the Battle of Antietam, where 23,000 soldiers lost their lives in the Civil War; thought to be the turning point of the war in favor of the Union. (t. 74)

Appalachian Mountain Region (ap′ ə lā′ chən moun′ tən rē′ jən) Area covering the western part of the state that has the highest elevations. (m. 13, t. 13)

Appalachian Mountains (ap′ ə lā′ chən moun′ təns) Mountain system running through the eight states in the southeastern part of the United States. (t. 18)

Atlantic Coastal Plain Region (at lan′ tik kō′ stl plān rē′ jən) Area covering more than half the state, including Chesapeake Bay and Baltimore; the eastern shore is wet and marshy, the western shore is slightly higher with more forests. (m. 13, t. 13)

B

Backbone Mountain (bak′ bōn moun′ tən) Highest location in Maryland, rising 3,360 feet above sea level; located in the Allegheny Mountains. (t. 8)

Baltimore (bȯl′ tə môr) One of the nation's busiest seaports, and largest city in Maryland; located on Chesapeake Bay; 39°N, 76°W. (t. 7)

Battle of Long Island (bat′ l ȯv lȯng ī′ lənd) Site of battle where Marylanders, known as the "troops of the line," protected General Washington's troops as they retreated in defeat. (t. 61)

Blackwater National Wildlife Refuge (blak wȯ′ tər nash′ ə nəl wīld′ lif ref′ yüj) Area located in the wetlands of the Atlantic Coastal Plain region; it provides a safe home for endangered birds such as the bald eagle and peregrine falcon. (t. 14)

Blue Ridge Mountains (blü rij moun′ təns) Located in the eastern part of the Appalachian Mountain region and part of the Appalachian mountain system. (t. 18)

Bush River (bùsh riv′ ər) Flows through the Piedmont Plateau region, bringing water to the region's farmland and forests. (t. 16)

Bush River Basin (bùsh riv′ ər bā′ sn) Located in the Piedmont Plateau region, it is an example of how rivers flow through the area. (t. 16)

 **C**

Chesapeake and Ohio Canal (ches′ ə pēk′ and ō hi′ ō kə nal) Connecting Washington, D.C., and the Ohio River valley, construction on the canal began in 1828. (t. 69)

Chesapeake Bay (ches′ ə pēk′ bā) Divides Maryland into its eastern and western areas. (m. 7, 18, 68, t. 7)

Chesapeake Bay Bridge (ches′ ə pēk′ bā brij) Opened in 1952, allowing people to drive across the bay from Maryland's eastern shore to its western shore. (t. 10)

Chester Town (ches′ tər toun) (now known as Chestertown) Location of the Chester Town Tea Party, where colonists demonstrated for the British their refusal to pay taxes; 39°N, 76°W. (t. 59)

Conowingo Dam (kä nə win′ gō dam) Built on the Susquehanna River, it is one of the biggest hydroelectric producers in America. (t. 21)

Crisfield (kris′ fēld) Small eastern shore town that hosts the National Hard Shelled Crab Derby and Fair; known by Marylanders as the "seafood capital of the world"; 38°N, 76°W. (t. 21)

Cumberland (kum′ bər lənd) Located on the Potomac River; the location where the National Road began in the 1800s; 39°N, 79°W. (t. 19, 68)

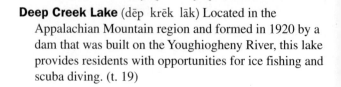 **D**

Deep Creek Lake (dēp krēk lāk) Located in the Appalachian Mountain region and formed in 1920 by a dam that was built on the Youghiogheny River, this lake provides residents with opportunities for ice fishing and scuba diving. (t. 19)

Delmarva Peninsula (del mär′ və pə nin′ sə lə) Name of Eastern Shore area, its name comes from the states of Delaware, Maryland, and Virginia; much of the peninsula is wet and marshy. (t. 14)

Fort McHenry (fôrt mək hen′ rē) Located in Baltimore; site upon which British ships fired on September 13, 1814; inspiration for Francis Scott Key's poem, "Defense of Fort McHenry," which became the words to our national anthem. 39°N, 76°W. (t. 66)

Fort McHenry Tunnel (fôrt mək hen′ rē tun′ l) Underwater tunnel that allows people to travel under Baltimore Harbor. (t. 11)

Great Falls (grāt fȯlz) White water area on the Potomac River, marking the fall line between the Piedmont Plateau region and the Atlantic Coastal Plain region. (t. 16)

Havre de Grace (ha vər də gras′) Birthplace of baseball legend Cal Ripkin, Jr., one of the best shortstops in history; 39°N, 76°W. (t. 135)

Mason-Dixon Line (mā′ sn dik′ sən lin) A 233-mile boundary line dividing Maryland from Pennsylvania and Delaware (t. 54, m. 54)

National Road (nash′ ə nəl rōd) First federally funded highway in the United States; originally connected Cumberland, Maryland, to Wheeling, West Virginia. (m. 68, t. 68)

Ocean City (ō′ shən sit′ ē) Located on the coast of the Atlantic Ocean; 38°N, 75°W. (t. 9)

Piedmont Plateau Region (pēd′ mont pla tō′ rē′ jən) Area in the center of the state; it is higher than the land in the east but lower than the land in the west; the Potomac River flows through this region to the Great Falls. (m. 13, t. 13)

Potomac River (pə tō′ mək riv′ ər) The 400-mile long Potomac begins in West Virginia, flows through Washington, D.C., and empties into Chesapeake Bay. (t. 16)

Preakness® Stakes (prēk′ nəs stāks) Week-long celebration in Baltimore honoring Maryland's horseracing tradition. (t. 127)

St. Clement's Island (sānt klem′ ənts ī′ lənd) Landing point of the *Ark* and the *Dove,* ships that brought English settlers to Maryland in 1633, where the travelers held Thanksgiving. (m. 53, t. 53)

St. Mary's City (sant mâr′ ēz sit ē) First European settlement located on the Western Shore of Maryland, and the state's first capital; 38°N, 76°W. (t. 54)

Salisbury (salz′ ber ē) One of the biggest cities on the Eastern Shore, and home to some of the state's largest producers of chicken; 38°N, 76°W. (t. 23)

Washington, D.C. (wash′ ing tən dē sē) Nation's capital, located in the District of Columbia and bordering Virginia and Maryland; 39°N, 77°W. (t. 63)

Youghiogheny River (yäk′ ə gā′ nē riv′ ər) Nicknamed the "Yock River," it is Maryland's first wild river providing recreation and outdoor adventure opportunities. (t. 19)

Pronunciation Key

a in hat	ō in open	sh in she
ā in age	ȯ in all	th in thin
â in care	ô in order	ᴛʜ in then
ä in far	oi in oil	zh in measure
e in let	ou in out	ə = a in about
ē in equal	u in cup	ə = e in taken
ėr in term	u̇ in put	ə = i in pencil
i in it	ü in rule	ə = o in lemon
ī in ice	ch in child	ə = u in circus
o in hot	ng in long	

Biographical Dictionary

This biographical dictionary tells you about people in this book and how to pronounce their names. The page number tells you where the person first appears in the text.

Banneker, Benjamin (ban′ ə ker) 1731–1806 Early African American inventor; helped design Washington, D.C. (p. 122)

Bell, Robert M. (bel) b. 1943 First African American to hold the position of Chief Judge on the Maryland Court of Appeals. (p. 99)

Blake, Eubie (blāk) 1883–1983 Musician and composer of ragtime music. (p. 123)

Booth, John Wilkes (büth) 1838–1865 Shot President Abraham Lincoln. (p. 75)

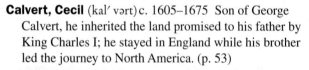

Calvert, Cecil (kal′ vərt) c. 1605–1675 Son of George Calvert, he inherited the land promised to his father by King Charles I; he stayed in England while his brother led the journey to North America. (p. 53)

Calvert, George (kal′ vərt) c. 1580–1632 Roman Catholic who wanted to escape religious persecution asked King Charles I for permission to start a colony north of the Potomac River. (p. 52)

Calvert, Leonard (kal′ vərt) 1606–1647 Son of George Calvert and brother of Cecil Calvert; led about 150 people from England to the Maryland colony. (p. 53)

Carroll, Charles (kar′ əl) 1737–1832 Marylander who signed the Declaration of Independence and helped form Maryland's government and constitution; elected to serve as senator in 1781. (pp. 60–61)

Carroll, Daniel (kar′ əl) 1730–1796 Marylander who signed the Constitution of the United States. (p. 62)

Chase, Samuel (chās) 1741–1811 Marylander who signed the Declaration of Independence and served as a state judge. (pp. 60–61)

Claiborne, William (klā′ bərn) 1587–1677 European who arrived in Chesapeake Bay in 1621 and settled on Kent Island; established a trading post there. (p. 52)

Clancy, Tom (klan′ sē) 1947– Maryland author who writes suspense and mystery novels. (p. 137)

Dixon, Jeremiah (dik′ sən) 1733–1779 With Charles Mason, spent four years surveying to help settle the dispute over Maryland's boundary, creating the Mason-Dixon Line. (p. 54)

Douglass, Frederick (dug′ ləs) 1818–1895 African American known for his work to end slavery. (p. 122)

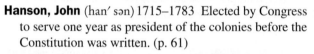

Fritchie, Barbara (frit′ chē) 1766–1862 Marylander who protected the flag in Frederick during the Civil War. (p. 127)

Hanson, John (han′ sən) 1715–1783 Elected by Congress to serve one year as president of the colonies before the Constitution was written. (p. 61)

Henson, Matthew (hen′ sən) 1866–1955 African American member of an expedition to reach the North Pole. (p. 122)

Holiday, Billie (hol′ ə dā) 1915–1959 Celebrated as one of America's greatest female jazz singers. (p. 123)

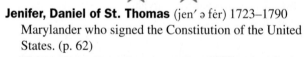

Jenifer, Daniel of St. Thomas (jen′ ə fėr) 1723–1790 Marylander who signed the Constitution of the United States. (p. 62)

Johnston, Joshua (jon′ stən) ?–1830 First nationally recognized African American portrait painter. (p. 123)

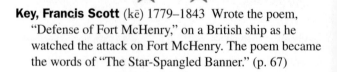

Key, Francis Scott (kē) 1779–1843 Wrote the poem, "Defense of Fort McHenry," on a British ship as he watched the attack on Fort McHenry. The poem became the words of "The Star-Spangled Banner." (p. 67)

L

Lee, General Robert E. (lē) 1807–1870 Commander of the army of the Confederacy. (p. 74)

Lincoln, Abraham (ling′ kən) 1809–1865 President of the United States; sent Union soldiers to Maryland to protect it from Confederate soldiers. (p. 73)

M

Marshall, Thurgood (mär′ shəl) 1908–1993 The first African American to serve on the U.S. Supreme Court. (p. 99)

Mason, Charles (mā′ sn) 1730–1787 With Jeremiah Dixon, spent four years surveying to help settle the dispute over Maryland's boundary, creating the Mason-Dixon Line. (p. 54)

McHenry, James (mək hen′ rē) 1753–1816 Marylander, who signed the Constitution of the United States. (p. 62)

P

Paca, William (pä′ kä) 1740–1799 Marylander who signed the Declaration of Independence. (p. 60)

Peale, Charles Willson (pēl) 1741–1827 Leading portrait artist during his time; painted an early portrait of George Washington; helped start the Pennsylvania Academy of Fine Arts, the oldest art school in the country. (p. 133)

Pickersgill, Mary (pik′ ėrz gil) 1776–1857 Made the flag that was raised at Fort McHenry. (p. 67)

Poe, Edgar Allan (pō) 1809–1849 One of Maryland's most famous authors; died in Baltimore in 1849. (p. 70)

R

Ripken, Cal, Jr. (rip′ kən) b. 1960 One of the best shortstops in baseball history, now retired; coaches camps for youths. (p. 135)

Roosevelt, Franklin Delano (rō′ zə velt) 1882–1945 Became President of the United States during the Great Depression; launched the New Deal. (p. 85)

S

Smith, John (smith) 1579?–1631 British explorer who settled Jamestown, Virginia, and then explored Chesapeake Bay. (p. 52)

Stewart, Anthony 1700s (stü′ ərt) Merchant who owned the ship *Peggy Stewart,* and sailed it into Baltimore Harbor with a cargo and of tea. Colonists, angry about the English tea tax, frightened him so badly that he apologized and set the ship on fire. (p. 59)

Stone, Thomas (stōn) Marylander who signed the Declaration of Independence. (p. 60)

T

Tubman, Harriet (tub mən) c. 1820–1913 Conductor on the Underground Railroad who escaped enslavement but returned to help others escape. (p. 73)

Tyler, Anne (tī′ lėr) b. 1941 Pulitzer Prize-winning author from Baltimore. (p. 135)

U

Unitas, Johnny (yü ni′ təs) 1933–2002 Quarterback and football hero who led the Baltimore Colts to three championships and one Super Bowl victory. (p. 135)

V

Verrazano, Giovanni (ver′ ə zä′ nō) 1485–1528 Italian explorer who, in 1524, may have been the first European to sail through Chesapeake Bay. (p. 52)

Pronunciation Key		
a in hat	ō in open	sh in she
ā in age	ȯ in all	th in thin
â in care	ô in order	ᴛʜ in then
ä in far	oi in oil	zh in measure
e in let	ou in out	ə = a in about
ē in equal	u in cup	ə = e in taken
ėr in term	u̇ in put	ə = i in pencil
i in it	ü in rule	ə = o in lemon
ī in ice	ch in child	ə = u in circus
o in hot	ng in long	

This glossary will help you understand and pronounce the terms and vocabulary words in this book. The page number tells you where the word first appears.

★ A ★

absentee ballot (ab′ sən tē′ bal′ ət) A way of casting a vote when unable to go to the polling location. (p. 108)

anthem (an′ thəm) Song of praise. (p. 67)

artifact (är′ tə fakt) Anything made by humans. (p. 49)

artisan (är′ tə zən) Skilled craftsworker. (p. 130)

★ B ★

ballot (bal′ ət) A way of casting a secret vote. (p. 108)

bill (bil) Proposed state law. (p. 95)

blockade (blo kād′) A way of controlling what goes in and out of an area. (p. 65)

★ C ★

cannery (kan′ ər ē) Factory where food is canned. (p. 81)

Chesapeake blockade (ches′ ə pēk′ blo kād′) Blockade set up in Chesapeake Bay by British ships; helped start the War of 1812. (p. 65)

citizen (sit′ ə zən) Person who by birth or by choice is a member of a nation. (p. 96)

coastal plain (kō′ stl plān) Flat land near an ocean. (p. 14)

crab pot (krab pot) Trap for catching crabs. (p. 128)

★ D ★

decoy (dē koi) Carved wooden statue. (p. 128)

deforestation (dē fôr is tā′ shən) Removal of trees. (p. 26)

Delmarva Peninsula (del mär′ və pə nin′ sə lə) Area named for Delaware, Maryland, and Virginia. (p. 14)

depression (di presh′ ən) Period of economic difficulty that results in lost jobs. (p. 85)

diversity (də vėr′ sə tē) Variety. (p. 120)

★ E ★

emancipation (i man′ sə pā′ shən) To free from slavery. (p. 74)

estuary (es′ chü er′ ē) Coastal waterway in which freshwater and seawater mix. (p. 10)

★ F ★

fall line (fȯl lin) Edge of a plateau. (p. 13)

First Continental Congress (fėrst kon′ tə nen′ tl kong′ gris) Group of representatives from the colonies seeking fair treatment from Britain. (p. 59)

fisher (fish′ ər) Person who hunts for fish. (p. 42)

★ G ★

General Assembly (jen′ ər əl ə sem′ blē) Legislative body that makes the laws in certain states. (p. 93)

general election (jen′ ər əl i lek′ shən) Election in which voters choose government officials. (p. 108)

governor (guv′ ər nər) Head of the state executive branch. (p. 93)

★ H ★

habitat (hab′ ə tat) Home for animals, plants, fish, or other living things. (p. 26)

high-tech (hī′ tek′) Using advanced technology. (p. 11)

House of Delegates (hous ov del′ ə gits) One of two houses in Maryland's legislature. (p. 93)

hydroelectric (hī′ drō i lek′ trik) Producing water-generated electricity. (p. 21)

★ I ★

impressment (im pres′ mənt) Kidnapping and forcing sailors into military service. (p. 65)

indentured servant (in den′ chərd sėr′ vənt) Contract laborer. (p. 56)

independent city (in′ di pen′ dənt sit′ ē) City that operates its own government, such as Baltimore. (p. 93)

iron horse (ī′ ərn hôrs) Steam locomotive. (p. 69)

★ J ★

jousting (jous′ ting) Sport in which riders on horseback try to put lances through a ring; state sport of Maryland. (p. 134)

lacrosse (lə krȯs) Team sport in which players attempt to knock a rubber ball past a goalie and into a net using a stick with a basket on the end. (p. 134)

longshoreman (lȯng′ shôr mən) Worker who loads and unloads ships. (p. 44)

marsh (märsh) Watery area covered in grass. (p. 9)

Mason-Dixon Line (mā′ sn dik′ sən lin) Line that divides Maryland from Pennsylvania and Delaware. (p. 54)

militia (mə lish′ ə) Army of citizens. (p. 66)

mountain system (moun tən sis′ təm) Area of mountain ridges, meadows, and valleys. (p. 18)

National Road (nash ə nəl rōd) First federally funded highway in the United States. (p. 68)

persecution (pėr′ sə kyü′ shən) Bad treatment. (p. 52)

petition (pə tish′ ən) To request change, usually from someone in authority. (p. 107)

piedmont (pēd′ mont) At the foot of a mountain. (p. 16)

pollution (pə lü′ shən) Material that dirties the environment. (p. 26)

population density (pop′ yə lā′ shən dən′ sə tē) Number of people living on a measured area of land. (p. 119)

primary election (prī′ mer′ ē ē lek′ shən) Election in which voters choose candidates for an upcoming general election. (p. 108)

privateer (prī′ və tir′) Citizen-owned armed ships. (p. 61)

Project Citizen (proj′ ekt sit′ ə zən) Education program that teaches Maryland students about citizenship. (p. 109)

★ S ★

Second Continental Congress (sek′ ənd kon′ tə nen′ tl kong′ gris) Group of representatives from the colonies who signed the Declaration of Independence. (p. 60)

secretary (sek′ rə ter′ ē) Head of a state department. (p. 94)

Senate (sen′ it) In Maryland, one of two houses of the state legislature. (p. 93)

service industry (sėr′ vis in′ də strē) Providing services rather than products. (p. 33)

shoreline (shôr′ lin′) Where land meets water. (p. 7)

Smart Growth Campaign (smärt grōth cam pān′) Program whose purpose is to plan growth in Maryland. (p. 100)

Stamp Act (stamp akt) A form of tax requiring colonists to buy stamps for newspapers and legal papers. (p. 59)

strike (strik) Stop work in protest. (p. 70)

subcabinet (sub kab′ ə nit) Specialized Maryland cabinet, such as Children, Youth, and Family. (p. 94)

swamp (swämp) Wet area similar to a marsh but with tall trees instead of grasses. (p. 9)

term (tėrm) Period of time spent serving in office. (p. 94)

tolerance (tol′ ər əns) Respect for others. (p. 52)

Townsend Acts (toun′ shənd akts) British tax on glass, paper, tea in American colonies. (p. 59)

Treaty of Paris (trē tē ov par′ is) Document that finalized the peace agreement between Great Britain and the United States following the American Revolution. (p. 62)

tree community (trē kə myü′ nə tē) Trees needing similar soil and climate conditions. (p. 24)

veto (vē′ tō) Governor's refusal to sign a bill. (p. 95)

vote (vōt) To choose a government official by election. (p. 108)

watershed (wȯ′ tər shed′) All of the rivers and streams that flow into a body of water such as a bay. (p. 26)

wigwam (wig′ wäm) Native American house. (p. 50)

Pronunciation Key

a in hat	ō in open	sh in she
ā in age	ȯ in all	th in thin
â in care	ô in order	ᴛʜ in then
ä in far	oi in oil	zh in measure
e in let	ou in out	ə = a in about
ē in equal	u in cup	ə = e in taken
ėr in term	u̇ in put	ə = i in pencil
i in it	ü in rule	ə = o in lemon
ī in ice	ch in child	ə = u in circus
o in hot	ng in long	

Index/Credits

This index lists the page numbers on which topics appear in this book. Page numbers after an *m* refer to maps. Page numbers after a *c* refer to charts and graphs. Page numbers after a *p* refer to photographs.

Credits

TEXT

MAPS
MapQuest.com, Inc.

ILLUSTRATIONS
18 Elizabeth Wolf; 50 Derek Grinnell; 104 Greg Harris; 123 Dan Krovatin

PHOTOGRAPHS
Every effort has been made to secure permission and provide appropriate credit for photographic material. The publisher deeply regrets any omission and pledges to correct errors called to its attention in subsequent editions.

Unless otherwise acknowledge, all photographs are the property of Scott Foresman, a division of Pearson Education.

Photo locators denoted as follows: Top (T), Center (C), Bottom (B), Left (L), Right (R), Background (Bkgd)

COVER: (c) ©Charles E. Pefley/Mira.com, (Bkgd) ©David C. Tomlinson/Getty Images **FRONT MATTER:** iii The Granger Collection, New York; 1 The Granger Collection, New York; 2 Richard Rowan, Photo Researchers, Inc.; 3 (cr) © David Ball/CORBIS, (tl) Catherine Karnow/Folio, Inc., (cl) © David Muench/CORBIS, (tr) © Leonard Rue Enterprises/ Animals Animals/Earth Scenes **CHAPTER 1:** 6 ©Tom Brakefield/CORBIS; 10 (tr) Greg Pease/Taxi/Getty Images, (b) ©Kevin Fleming/CORBIS; 11 Jeffrey A. Lubchansky; 12 ©Royalty-Free/CORBIS; 14 (b) ©Paul A. Souders/CORBIS, (tr) ©David Muench/CORBIS; 15 (tr) ©Rob & Ann Simpson/Visuals Unlimited, (cl) ©Royalty-Free/CORBIS; 16 (t) ©Kevin Fleming/CORBIS, (br) ©Mark Gibson/Visuals Unlimited; 17 (bc) Anthony Mercieca/Photo Researchers, Inc., (cr) From the Collection of the Office of the Maryland Secretary of State; 18 ©Paul A. Souders/CORBIS; 19 ©Paul A. Souders/CORBIS; 20 ©Lowell Georgia/CORBIS; 21 (t) ©Paul A. Souders/CORBIS, (cr) ©James L. Amos/CORBIS; 23 (cr) ©Richard T. Nowitz/Photo Researchers, Inc., (c) ©BARRY RUNK/Grant Heilman Photography, Inc., (bl) ©Randy Miller/CORBIS, (br) Edwin Remsberg/Stone/Getty Images; 24 ©Paul A. Souders/CORBIS; 25 ©Reuters/CORBIS; 26 Mary Hollinger, NODC Biologist, Courtesy of the National Oceanic and Atmospheric Administration Central Library Photo Collection; 27 ©Paul A. Souders/CORBIS; 28 ©Royalty-Free/CORBIS; 29 ©Paul A. Souders/CORBIS; 30 Chris Conner / Chesapeake Bay Program; 31 Mary Hollinger, NODC biologist, Courtesy of the National Oceanic and Atmospheric Administration Central Library Photo Collection; 32 Jeffrey F. Bill/The Baltimore Zoo; 33 (bc) ©Michael Newman/PhotoEdit, Inc., (br) ©Tom Carter/PhotoEdit, Inc., (cr) ©Richard T. Nowitz/CORBIS; 34 ©Roger Ressmeyer/CORBIS; 35 (bl) ©Robert Maass/CORBIS, (cr) Photodisc Blue/Getty Images, (bc) ©Jeffrey L. Rotman/CORBIS; 36 Stone/Getty Images; 37 ©Richard T. Nowitz/CORBIS; 38 Lance C. Bell

AAD-INC.; 39 (bl) Henry Horenstein/Stock Boston, (tr) ©Paul A. Souders/CORBIS; 40 (b) ©Ric Ergenbright/CORBIS, (cr) ©Royalty-Free/CORBIS; 41 ©Robert Dowling/CORBIS; 42 ©Paul A. Souders/CORBIS; 43 (bl) ©Owen Franken/CORBIS, (tr) ©James L. Amos/CORBIS; 44 (tr) Greg Pease/The Image Bank/Getty Images, (b) ©Paul A. Souders/CORBIS; 48 (bl) Boden/Ledingham/Masterfile **CHAPTER 2:** 49 ©Lowell Georgia/CORBIS; 50 © 1998 R. Nowitz Photos Ltd/ Courtesy of Historic St. Mary's City; 52 The Maryland Historical Society, Baltimore, Maryland; 55 (b) Hulton Archive/Getty Images, (c, cr, tr) Historic Saint Mary's City; 56 Carolyn Merchant; 57 (br) ©Bettmann/CORBIS, (cl) ©Stapleton Collection/CORBIS, (bkgd) The Granger Collection, New York; 59 (b) © 1998. Kent County Office of Tourism Development., (tc) Library of Congress; 60 (b) ©Bettmann/CORBIS, (cl) ©SuperStock, Inc./SuperStock; 61 Library of Congress, Prints & Photographs Division, LC-USZC4-6294; 62 (bl) ©CORBIS, (cr) ©Robert Maass/CORBIS, (b) ©Lowell Georgia/CORBIS; 63 (cr) Hulton Archive/Getty Images, (c) ©CORBIS; 64 Picture History; 65 Picture History; 67 Courtesy of Gallon Historical Art, Gettysburg, PA, www.gallon.com; 69 (tr) The Maryland Historical Society, Baltimore, Maryland, (br) History Magazine/Harpers Magazine; 70 (tc) The Granger Collection, New York, (cl) Hulton Archive/Getty Images; 71 (br) ©North Wind/North Wind Picture Archives, (cl) AP/Wide World Photos, (bkgd) ©Ron Watts/CORBIS; 72 ©Tria Giovan/CORBIS; 74 Hulton Archive/Getty Images; 75 (cl) Dorling Kindersley, (cl) Larry Sherer/High Impact Photography; 76 Library of Congress, Prints & Photographs Division, LC-USZC4-1526; 77 (cl) The Charleston Museum, (br) The Granger Collection, New York, (bkgd) The Granger Collection, New York; 79 ©Dennis MacDonald/PhotEdit, Inc.; 80 PhotoDisc/Getty Images; 81 Courtesy of the Maryland State Archives, Special Collections (Robert G. Merrick Archives of Maryland Historical Photographs) MSA SC 1477-1-6181; 82 Harper's Weekly, Courtesy of the Chesapeake Bay Maritime Museum; 83 Library of Congress; 84 ©Hulton-Deutsch Collection/CORBIS; 85 (br) The Granger Collection, New York, (b) Harry Todd/Hulton Archives/Getty Images; 86 (cr) Richard Anderson, (cl) ©Paul A. Souders/CORBIS, (b) ©Mark E. Gibson/CORBIS; 88 (tc) U.S. Air Force, (tr) Winterthur Museum, (b) Maryland Office of Tourism Development, (cl) Courtesy of the Federal Highway Administration; 89 (cr) ©Joe Feingersh/Stock Market/CORBIS, (t) Rockwell/Tsado/Tom Stack & Associates, Inc., (c) ©Index Stock/Alamy, (br) Ryan McVay/Photodisc green/Getty Images, (bl) Michael Freeman, (t) NASA **CHAPTER 3:** 92 Steve Gorton/Dorling Kindersley; 95 (tr) ©Michael Pole/CORBIS, (cr) ©Anne Griffiths Belt/CORBIS, (b) ©Paul A. Souders/CORBIS; 96 ©Lowell Georgia/CORBIS; 97 ©Paul Conklin/PhotoEdit, Inc.; 98 AFP/Getty Images; 100 (bl) Howard County Library, (br) Henry Aldrich/Aldrich Photo; 102 ©Paul A. Souders/CORBIS; 103 (br) Cynthia Johnson/Time Life Pictures/Getty Images, (cl) Thurgood Marshall Scholarship Fund, (bkgd) Robert Harbison; 105 ©Paul Conklin/PhotoEdit, Inc.; 107 (b) ©Steve Rubin/The Image Works, (tr) AP/Wide World Photos; 108 ©Tom Carter/PhotoEdit, Inc.; 109 (tl) Russell Kaye/Stone/Getty Images,